First published in the U.K. in 1983 by Blandford Press,
Link House, West Street, Poole, Dorset BH15 1LL

This edition published 1986 by New Orchard Editions Ltd
Robert Rogers House
New Orchard
Poole, Dorset BH15 1LU

© 1983 Blandford Press Ltd

ISBN 1 85079 038 8

Distributed in the USA by Sterling Publishing Co.Inc,
2 Park Avenue, New York, NY 10016

Distributed in Australia by
Capricorn Link (Australia) Pty Ltd
PO Box 665
Lane Cove, NSW 2066

Designed by Rob Burt
Produced by Charles Herridge Ltd
Printed in Yugoslavia by
CGP Delo, Ljubljana

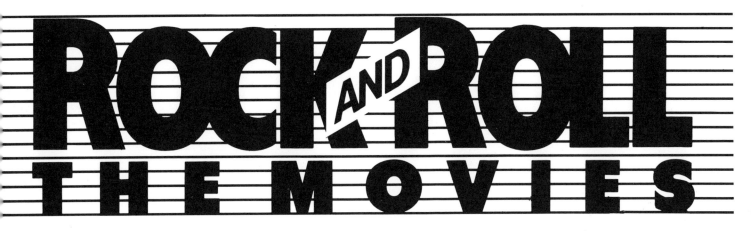

ROCK AND ROLL THE MOVIES

Rob Burt

NEW ORCHARD EDITIONS
POOLE · NEW YORK · SYDNEY

I remember it was a wet Saturday afternoon – I must have been about eight or nine years old – when my big sister Geraldine dragged me along to the Cinema to see Elvis in *Jailhouse Rock*. As a sign of gratitude I dedicate this book to her and to the memory of Elvis Presley and John Arvanities – who first played me 'Wipe Out'.

About the Author

Designer, journalist and album compiler Rob Burt's books include *The Illustrated Rock Quiz, The Illustrated Movie Quiz Book* and *The Tube*. A bold rider of the wavy line he has contributed surfing entries to *The Caxton Encyclopedia* and *Walt Disney's Sport Goofy Encyclopedia*.

Contents

From The King to Sting and Kookie to The Fonz and The Wild One to Quadrophenia

AISLE JIVIN':
Are these our children?

TOWN SITS ON ROCK 'N' ROLL VOLCANO — RHYTHM-CRAZED TEENAGERS TERRORIZE A CITY — ROCK 'N' ROLL RIOTS FLARE UP AGAIN blared the headlines.
What went wrong? asked the newspapers, churches and police forces. "Are these our children?" asked the parents, school teachers and civic leaders.
"Rock and Roll is here to stay," cried a generation who dismissed convention, broke the rules and changed the way kids dressed, danced and behaved for all-time.

Juvenile delinquency and mixed-up kids kept the fifties press turning with sensational reports of rock 'n' roll revolts and general teenage unrest — a blanket coverage from Boston to Bolton, with most of the blame put squarely at the feet of rock movies.

One thing is for sure, without movies rock 'n' roll might never have left first base. Hollywood in the fifties was quick to sense a change of mood and audience, and started promoting images and idols ready made for the new teenage market.

The young could not help but identify with Marlon Brando's leather-clad leader-of-the-gang in *The Wild One* (1954) or James Dean's over-sensitive, new-kid-in-town in *Rebel Without a Cause* (1955), both gifted performances in milestone movies. Although both movies were based on rock culture, neither included rock 'n' roll music — *The Wild One*'s soundtrack featured jazz performed by Shorty Rogers and his Giants while Leonard Rosenman's *Rebel* score was pure cinema city symphony.

If *The Wild One* was the touch paper and *Rebel* the spark, then *Blackboard Jungle* (1955) became the explosion — a great explosion that was to be felt around the world. On the face of it *Blackboard Jungle* looked like a typical Hollywood melodrama set in a tough New York school, with an idealistic young teacher bending over backwards to win the hearts and minds of his delinquent charges. The magic formula that created the blast was director Richard Brooks' choice of Bill Haley's rock 'n' roll song "Rock Around the Clock" to open the film.

Bill Haley, the man once dubbed "least likely", was born in a Detroit suburb in 1927. A keen musician from an early age, he went on to make a good living from local radio, while fronting a country music band, the Saddlemen. After years of musical experiments Haley renamed his band the Comets and came up with his version of rock 'n' roll. He soon had a number of hit records behind him, many with teenage jive titles like "Crazy Man Crazy", "Shake Rattle and Roll", "See You Later Alligator" and "Hot Dog Buddy Buddy".

In 1954 he released the single "Rock Around the Clock". Described at the time as a "novelty foxtrot", it quietly sank without a chart placing. Then, luckily for Bill, Richard Brooks picked up on the song while adapting Evan Hunter's slum school book for the screen, and later added it to the film's soundtrack, along with jazz tunes by such luminaries as Stan Kenton and Bix Beiderbecke. Teenagers all over America flocked to the movie and soon sent Haley's rock anthem straight to the top of the charts.

Shrewd Hollywood B movie veterans Sam Katzman and Fred Sears noted the impact "Rock Around the Clock" made on the movie and quickly signed Bill and his song, added a bland script and produced the first of the rock 'n' roll quickies, *Rock Around the Clock* (1956). Script and acting ability aside, the movie was a huge success. Costing around $200,000 it later grossed $1,000,000 in the US alone.

Its impact on the rest of the world was as well documented as World War II itself and caused almost as much damage judging by many press reports. In Britain the papers reported teddy boys jiving in the aisles, tearing up cinema seats and behaving like hooligans; Egypt called it an American plot "designed to sow trouble in the Middle East by undermining Egyptian morale"; Moscow condemned it, while in Iran it was described as "a threat to civilization". By the time these rave reviews appeared in the world's press, Katzman, Sears, Haley and Co. had already completed the follow-up with a title that seemed to answer their critics — *Don't Knock the Rock* (1957).

These movies not only introduced the new beat to a world audience, but surprisingly made the rotund, kiss-curled bopper rock 'n' roll's biggest star. Alas, Bill's run as a top rock screen attraction was short-lived, lasting only a few months. The reason was as obvious as his plaid jacket — for in 1956 the boy with the weird name from Tupelo, Mississippi also hit the screen.

This was a bumper year for rock movies, not only producing *Rock Around the Clock* and Elvis Presley's film debut in *Love Me Tender*, but also the highly acclaimed movie *The Girl Can't Help It*. Produced, directed and co-written by Frank Tashlin, *The Girl Can't Help It* was set in the world of pop music and concerned a press agent's (Tom Ewell) attempts to hype a gangster's moll (Jayne Mansfield) to stardom.

To help the girl and the action along Tashlin used the then rare processes of colour and Cinemascope and injected some of the finest rock 'n' roll on celluloid, including classic performances from a gathering of rock's leading exponents and latest heartthrobs — Eddie Cochran, Little Richard, Gene Vincent, the Platters and Fats Domino among others. The movie has since been described as "the first worthwhile film to boast an array of rock stars", a view not shared by a critic of the day who described Little Richard as "a diminutive South Sea Islander who plays the piano standing up".

At best, *The Girl Can't Help It* provided a visual jukebox, making the new rock stars accessible to millions via movie houses throughout the world and also providing its young performers with their first Hollywood experience. Cochran and Vincent, for example, soon caught the acting bug; Eddie appeared in Howard Koch's cotton pickin' teen drama *Untamed Youth* (1957), while Gene turned up in the stock-car oater *Hot Rod Gang* (1958), one of the many movies combining rock 'n' roll, hot rods and drag racing. Gene Vincent and Eddie Cochran could have become even bigger screen idols if not for a fatal auto accident in 1960, in which Cochran lost his life and Vincent was seriously injured. Gene Vincent did, however, make a couple of movie appearances before his untimely death in 1971, but sadly they were only brief cameo spots.

Another young screen actor who met the same tragic end as both James Dean and Eddie Cochran was Brandon de Wilde. Born in 1942, this talented child star, probably best remembered as the boy who idolized gunfighter Alan Ladd in *Shane* (1953), went on to make a big impact with teen audiences in *Blue Denim* (1959). The movie dealt in a sensitive way with one of the more basic adolescent problems — two teenagers facing the consequences of an unwanted pregnancy, a welcome sign that Hollywood was exploring more than just the sensational teenage themes.

On the exploitive stage we were offered sex, drugs, rock 'n' roll and Mamie Van Doren in Jack Arnold's steamy *High School Confidential* (1958). Miss Van Doren's early publicity explained her rise to film stardom in these ever-so-slightly sexist terms: "How to be an actress in one easy lesson — learn to walk with an eye-catching swing!" It went on, "She hadn't done a test to prove she could act, she had never hit a note to prove she could sing. She just walked across the studio lot and every executive who saw her knew she should be in pictures."

An extremely colourful Hollywood scenario, but not quite accurate. It was, in fact, while singing in Las Vegas that Mamie (or Joan Lucille Olander, as she was originally known) was spotted by songwriter Jimmy McHugh. He encouraged her to study drama and she soon appeared on stage in a Los Angeles production of *Come Back Little Sheba*, where she came to the notice of Universal. Her film debut in *Forbidden* (1954) was followed by many screen appearances.

Mamie graduated from *High School Confidential* to *College Confidential* (1960) in which Steve Allan portrayed a small-town college professor charged with corrupting the morals of his pupils. By 1960 most youth-cult movies were featuring at least one recruit direct from the pop music charts and this time the honour fell to Conway "It's Only Make Believe" Twitty, who only months earlier had made his movie debut in *Platinum High School* (1959).

Some movies, such as *The Big Beat* (1957), had been even more ambitious, boasting not one, but a host of rock 'n' rollers. Disc jockey Alan Freed (the man who claimed to have invented the term rock 'n' roll) headed a series of these cheapies that were packed wall to wall with rock stars. *Rock, Rock, Rock* (1957), for example, featured Chuck Berry, Frankie Lymon and the Teenagers and the only screen appearance of the Johnny Burnette Trio. While Little Richard, Brook Benton and Laverne Baker were among the reelers 'n' rockers in *Mister Rock and Roll* (1957).

The very astute Freed had been in rock 'n' roll movies from the start. It was reported he had asked $15,000 for his role in *Rock Around the Clock* but the movie company offered him a percentage. He wasn't very happy with the offer, but took the advice of agent, Jolly Joyce, and accepted the percentage plus a small amount up front. His slice of the movie eventually made him a small fortune.

The best of his celluloid rock packages, *Go, Johnny, Go* (1959), which he financed himself, starred Chuck Berry in his acting debut plus an appearance by the soon-to-die Ritchie Valens. The movie was released the year Freed's career went into a sharp decline. He was declared bankrupt after paying huge legal costs to get off a charge of incitement to riot and anarchy. The action was brought after a near riot followed his rock 'n' roll show in Boston. This drama was quickly eclipsed by his involvement in the infamous US payola scandal, and his final fall came via a demand for back taxes that was unresolved at the time of his death in 1965.

Other movies of the teen hot rod rock 'n' roll genre continued to trundle out of the backlot, blazing a trail into the mid-sixties. A typical title was *Teenage Thunder* (1961) whose synopsis warned: "A lesson to all fathers who are reluctant to let their teenage sons have hot rods" — in this case the boy steals cars, drives to the danger of the public and generally plays hell.

All good clean teenage fun. This particular auto saga was directed by Paul Holinick and starred Charles Courtney, Melinda Byron and TV's *Laramie* star Robert Fuller as the bad guy.

This small acre of teen sub-culture became even more popular with a renewed interest created by such sixties groups as the Beach Boys, Rip Chords, Jan and Dean, and Ronny and the Daytones who raced up the charts with a string of sunlit hot rod songs including "Little Deuce Coupe", "Hey Little Cobra", "Deadman's Curve" and "G.T.O".

Sadly, this new found enthusiasm was not the case in the general rock 'n' roll circus, for Alan Freed's decline signalled a changing world. Many purists believed 1959 marked the end of the rock 'n' roll years, for within what seemed months Buddy Holly, Ritchie Valens, the Big Bopper and Eddie Cochran died, Chuck Berry went to prison, Jerry Lee Lewis was banned, Little Richard got religious and Elvis was drafted.

This year may have seen the exit of the original rock 'n' rollers as the top teenage attractions at the movies, but it also witnessed the rise of an altogether new band of well-groomed, well-capped and well-hyped screen favourites. This group was soon to take the teen idol symbol far beyond a young girl's wildest dreams.

Laslo Benedek's much banned *The Wild One* (1954) was the originator of the black boots and bike genre.
1 Marlon Brando played Johnny, the leader of a pack of Hell's Angels who terrorize a small town.

1

2

2 "What're you rebelling against?" asks Mary Murphy in the role of Kathy; "Whatta ya got?" replies Brando.

3 When Johnny's new-found affection for Little Miss Small Town is interpreted as weakness by big bad biker and pretender to his saddle, Lee Marvin, the two meet in a showdown in true western tradition. The movie, written by John Paxton, photographed by Hal Mohr and produced by Stanley Kramer, was finally given a British Board of Film Censors release certificate in 1967.

3

1 Nicholas Ray's all-time teen classic *Rebel Without a Cause* gave expression to the new culture and James Dean's performance established the teenage rebel image.
2 The film opens with new kid in town, Jim Stark (James Dean), lying wide-eyed and legless on the sidewalk. The unruly youth appears in his drunken state at Juvenile Hall where he meets Plato (Sal Mineo), a young delinquent.

3

3 After being questioned by the police, he reveals a deep disrespect for his domineering mother (Ann Doran) and weak-willed father (Jim Backus).
Also in trouble down at Juvenile Hall is Judy (Natalie Wood), a misunderstood teenager whom he runs into again the following morning on the way to school. At school he befriends Plato and makes an enemy of Judy's date, Buzz.
4 After a switchblade fight at a planetarium, Jim and Buzz decide to meet later that night for a duel, involving driving a couple of stolen motors on a chicken run to the edge of a cliff – the first to jump before the vehicles topple over the cliff is chicken. Jimmy rolls out of his sedan at the last second while Buzz, trapped by his jacket sleeve, plunges to his death.
5 Buzz's friends track Jim to a deserted mansion where he, Judy and Plato, armed with his father's gun, are hiding out. Plato opens fire at the gang. Hearing the shots, the police move in and Plato is accidentally gunned down, leaving a shattered first American teenager with a tear in his eye.

4

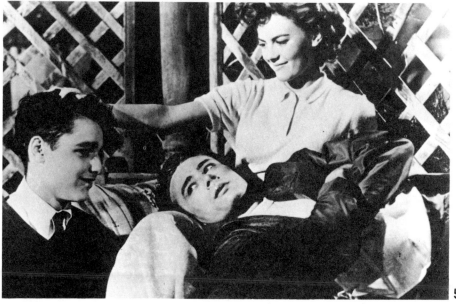

5

"When the titles flashed, Bill Haley and his Comets started blurching, 'One . . . Two . . . Three O'clock . . . Four O'clock Rock' . . . It was the loudest sound kids had ever heard at the time . . . Bill Haley . . . was playing the Teen-Age Anthem and he was loud. I was jumping up and down. *Blackboard Jungle,* not ever considering that it had the old people winning in the end, represented a strange act of 'endorsement' of the teenage cause . . ." This is how Frank Zappa remembered Richard Brooks' *The Blackboard Jungle* (1955) in a *Life* magazine article.

1 No apple for teacher. Glenn Ford's nice suit fails to impress his delinquent charges.
2 North Manual High School pupil Gregory W. Miller (Sidney Poitier) can just about be seen, second from left, silhouetted against the blackboard.

1

2

1 Bill Haley (1927-80) was to use his teen anthem again, dangling it like some great electric carrot, enticing the kids to part with their hard-earned pocket money in return for 74 mundane minutes of *Rock Around the Clock* (1955).

2 As if that wasn't enough, he soon jumped out of the frying pan into the deep freeze with *Don't Knock the Rock* (1956), the story of a rock 'n' roll star who returns to his home town to answer accusations of corrupting the kids with his music.

The hot rod/dragster genre thundered its way through Hollywood's celluloid strips.

1 Future Laramie TV star, John Smith (right), pats fellow small-screen westerner, Chuck Connors, on the back, while Lori Nelson looks on as if she really knows what goes phutt under the hood in Leslie Martinson's *Hot Rod Girl* (1956).

2 Car crazy cutie, Fay Spain, inspects the upholstery as boyfriend Steve Terrell thanks his lucky carbs he has a column shift in the dreary *Dragstrip Girl* (1957).

3 Hot rodders Steve Drexel, John Ashley, Jody Fair and Gene Vincent discuss yet another big drag in Lew Landers' *Hot Rod Gang* (1958). Vincent, who plays himself so well, also performs three songs in the movie.

4 Soon-to-be-surfer Bruce Johnston contributed to the soundtrack of *The Ghost of Dragstrip Hollow* (1959), where we find Russ Bender conducting a sweat-stained car club through a crash course in auto maintenance.

1

3

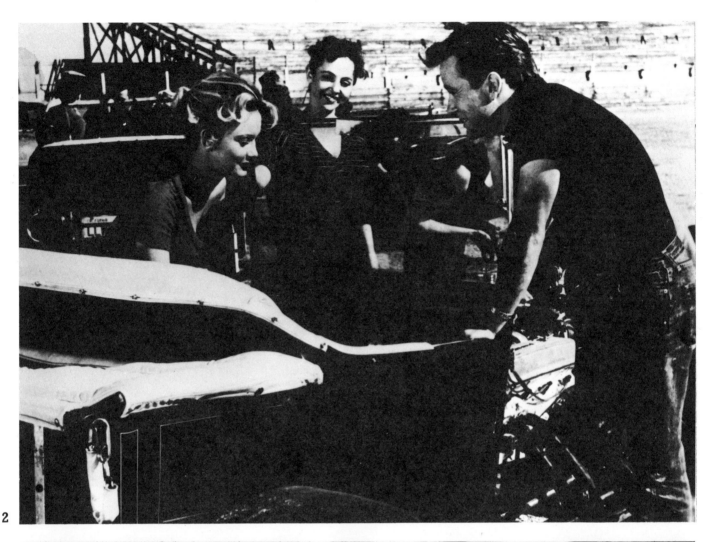

2

4

Back in class in Jack Arnold's *High School Confidential* (1958), the campus had become a world of sex, drugs and rock 'n' roll. The movie even included a government health warning.

1 Mamie Van Doren was outstanding as the prime sex interest.

2 Mamie's nephew, Russ Tamblyn, an undercover narcotics agent, plays it cool as John Drew Barrymore gets to grips with Jan Sterling.

3 Jerry Lee Lewis supplied some thumpin', jumpin' rock 'n' roll from the back of a truck for the opening number.

PAY LESS AT
RRY LEE LE
MUSIC TRUCK

1

2

3

4

5

6

4 Other young movie thugs, tearaways and troubled teenagers were to be found in *The Delinquents* (1957), a film that Robert Altman wishes he had never written, produced or directed. Richard Bakalyan and the gang look sleepily menacing.

5 Down on the correction farm, dog lover John Russell finds himself in a tight spot in Howard Koch's *Untamed Youth* (1957). The kid in the cap is Eddie Cochran.

6 A pubescent Carol Lynley is about to discover life's sweet mystery at the hands of a horny Brandon de Wilde in Philip Dunne's screen examination of a growing teenage problem in *Blue Denim* (1959).

1

2

"*The Girl Can't Help It* was the first film I can remember that was accepted as an A1 movie featuring blacks. It had Fats Domino, Little Richard and several other blacks and presented them in a beautiful way. I mean with a lot of class" – B. B. King. Frank Tashlin's *The Girl Can't Help It* (1956) is a much admired slice of rockerama.

1 Agent Tom Ewell nervously tries to restrain budding pop star Jayne Mansfield from doing something outrageous with her milk bottles.

2 The movie featured cherished cameos by some of rock 'n' roll's greatest names, including Gene Vincent, seen curbing a "real gone" Blue Cap (right) who seems hell bent on going over the top.

3 Also taking part in the venture were some bona fide Hollywood stars such as party pooper Edmond O'Brien.

4 Miss Mansfield's glamour and Mr Ewell's comedy played second fiddle to the rock 'n' roll content.

THE REBEL IMAGE:
From method to message

Marlon Brando and James Dean epitomized the new rebellious teenager, not only on the screen but off, with their legendary inability to come to terms with the star system and the typical studio stereotype Cinema City and the media demanded of them. This offbeat approach earned them a special place at the head of the rebels' top table. This nonconformist attitude was later adopted by other boat-rockers from the North of England's working class heroes to Hollywood's own silver spoon children — an uncompromising bunch who were bound together as Rebels without a Cause.

Marlon Brando

1 Marlon Brando, pictured in *On the Waterfront* (1954), mumbled his way through a host of outcast roles and spearheaded the line of Hollywood anti-heroes that followed. Ironically, the show-biz establishment that he rebelled against rewarded him time and time again with fame, fortune and Academy Awards.

2 Who would have believed that this paraplegic war veteran would lead a gang of Hell's Angels to the birth of rock 'n' roll? Brando in a scene from his debut movie, Fred Zinnemann's *The Men* (1950), featuring the starry-eyed Teresa Wright.

James Byron Dean (1931-55)

1 Part Peter Pan and part lost boy, James Dean was a truly original actor – a stylist who has often been imitated but never equalled as the screen's leading teenage rebel.

2 "Jesus Christ, he is Cal," exclaimed John Steinbeck. Jimmy played Cal Trask in his first major movie, *East of Eden* (1954), directed by Elia Kazan and based on the Steinbeck novel of the same name.

Kazan, describing his acting genius, commented "I felt that Dean's body was very graphic; it was almost writhing in pain sometimes. He was very twisted, almost like a cripple or a spastic of some kind."

3 His colleagues found him temperamental and moody. Richard Davalos (who portrayed his brother, Aron Trask) couldn't handle the situation and they were soon only speaking to each other in character on the set. It was a very different story with Julie Harris who played Abra (right). Kazan said "he was the luckiest guy in the world when he got Julie Harris to work with, because he could have gotten a girl that just got angry with him and castrated him. He was easily castrated; she was marvellous with him, took care of him, encouraged him and supported him."

His next movie should have been *Giant,* but shooting was put back a few months and he managed to fit in *Rebel Without a Cause* between assignments.

1

2

3

4 *Giant* (1955) sadly turned out to be his last movie. He played Jett Rink, a former ranch hand who strikes oil, and the way the script summed up the character could be interpreted as Jimmy's own epitaph: "A poor boy who makes a hundred million dollars. Tough, always angry, restless, bewildered and reckless, with an animal charm and tycoon's magnetism. He gets his way and loses his way with equal violence." James Dean died in an automobile accident, aged twenty four.

Natalie Wood (Natasha Gurdin, 1938-81)

The nearly always vulnerable Natalie was one of the few child stars to graduate to adult stardom.
1 Her childhood awards and achievements were endless, but it was her transitional role of Judy opposite James Dean in *Rebel Without a Cause* (1955) that clinched her first Oscar nomination.
2 *Rebel Without a Cause* was also reported to be Elvis Presley's favourite movie. Some say he even knew the dialogue word perfect, so what better way to spend an evening than dating Jimmy's girl.

3

3 Natalie made a couple of films with another fifties heartthrob, Tab Hunter. *The Burning Hills* (1956) found her in the Latin role of Maria, which gave her a wonderful opportunity to practise her accent.
4 The role certainly paid off. *West Side Story* (1961) co-directors, Robert Wise and Jerome Robbins, agreed that "if we wanted the ideal Maria, we wanted Natalie" and they signed her for the prestigious musical lead. Behind her magic movie persona Natalie projected just a hint of insecurity. Perhaps it was this trait – this little girl lost, whether to the Comanches or Warren Beatty – that went some way in explaining her highly individual off-screen life style.

4

Elvis Aaron Presley (1935-77)

"I began looking for excitement. You soon get bored with it. You start looking for something else . . . I admit I occasionally thought of being evil and getting into trouble just for kicks, but I managed to keep myself in check."

The pre-army Presley certainly cut a much more rebellious figure than the later demobbed King of Showbiz.

1 From a Memphis courthouse Elvis answers charges of assault. His "victims", pictured left, were a couple of redneck garage attendants.

2 The King enters Chicago's International Amphitheater to the roar of a capacity crowd.

3 Back home in Tupelo, he wows them at the state fair.

4 In later years the rebel spirit was occasionally let loose, if only to be caught in this neo-Brando pose.

3

4

Dean-alikes
Michael Parks

Michael Parks portrayed a host of post-Dean angry young men in a collection of mean and moody roles that would have made the original proud.

1 One of his best roles was that of a supertramp who guides young runaway Ceila Kaye to California in Brian Hutton's "arty yet gripping" *The Wild Seed* (1965).

2 He played the title role in Harvey Hart's small town opus *Bus Riley's Back in Town* (1965), based on a William Inge script and featuring a truly pure junior high heroine, Janet Margolin.

3 Parks stepped out of character in the off-beat and off-key caper *The Happening* (1967), with the lovely Faye Dunaway and the equally lovely George Maharis.

1

2

3

Martin Sheen

4 The spirit of Dean was recaptured by Martin Sheen as the 50s killer, Kit, in Terrence Malick's impressive directorial debut *Badlands* (1973).
5 It surfaced yet again in the character of Michael McCord, hero of Richard Heffron's hot-rodding auto saga *The California Kid* (1974).

1

2

Christopher Jones

Christopher Jones was hailed as yet
another successor to James Dean.
Perhaps his one-time father-in-law,
Lee Strasberg (founder of the famous
New York Actors' Studio, training
ground of Brando, Harris and Dean)
had some part in his sudden rise.
1 Jones never looked more like
Dean than in *Chubasco* (1968).
2 He was certainly at his rebel best
as the drug pushing millionaire pop
idol and presidential candidate Max
Frost in Barry Shear's *Wild in the
Streets* (1968). Produced by James
Nicolson and Sam Arkoff, the movie's
publicity had all the hallmarks of
typical A.I.P. teen exploitation . . .
"This is the story of Max Frost, 24 years
old . . . President of the United States
. . . who created the world in his own
image. To him, 30 is over the hill. 52%
of the nation is under 25 . . . and
they've got the power. That's how he
became President."
3 *Three in the Attic* (1968) found
young Chris all screwed up.
4 Despite their injuries, Chris and
Pia Degermark find plenty to laugh
about in *The Looking Glass War*
(1969).

2 Doing the Shadow shuffle in *The Young Ones* (1961).
3 Man from Nowhere doing the Hully Gully in *Just for Fun* (1963).

2

3

Jet Harris

1 Terence "Jet" Harris stepped out of the shadows and into the spotlight for what looked like the start of a promising solo career. Mean and moody, with a growing bass, he pushed a string of heavy and innovative singles into the charts before ill-health and misfortune made him a shadow of his former self.

The Fondas

The second wave of film star Fondas played their parts both on and off the screen – from Establishment to Anarchy in a single generation.

1 Hollywood's demure new princess shows the king of "Sunset Strip" round the set of her debut movie, *Tall Story* (1960).

2 Joshua Logan's tale of campus love and athletics (not necessarily in that order) finds Jane besotted, Anthony Perkins less certain.

3 From innocence to interplanetary striptease under the direction of husband Roger Vadim in *Barbarella* (1968). President of Paramount, Charles Bluhdorn, pronounced it an "absurd piece of trash" and ordered it to be written off as a disaster, a sentiment that Ms Fonda might well now echo.

4 As Bree Daniel in Alan J. Pakula's *Klute* (1971), Jane had a stab at playing a New York hooker in a performance that was sharp enough to win her an Academy Award.

Peter, who according to John Lennon knew what it was like to be dead, appeared in a number of movies that shared that knowledge with him. It was not until his association with Roger Corman that his career accelerated to a new high.

5 On the road to *Easy Rider* in *The Wild Angels* (1966), with Bruce Dern backing him up on the "buddy seat". Peter as Heavenly Blues took to the road where Brando's misunderstood Johnny left off. In doing so he brought to the screen a new insight into the problems facing the directionless young, when he declared at the end "There's nowhere to go".

6 Dennis "Kemo-sabay" Hopper first teamed up with Pete in Corman's *The Trip* (1967). Two years later, with a flash of light and a cloud of dust, they rode again in *Easy Rider*.

5

6

John Winston Lennon (1940-80)

"Kids are still more influenced by us than by Jesus Christ. As it happens, I'm very big on Jesus Christ" – John Lennon, 1969.

1 Always one to have the last word, John Lennon often expressed his revolutionary views via his music, adapting his sometimes very personal political slogans into a fine set of rock-song slogans, packed with catchy riffs and hooks.

2 Out of slumberland and into the Plastic Ono Band. John and Yoko as they appeared in D. A. Pennebaker's *Sweet Toronto* (1970).

3 During his sabbatical from Yoko, John was often found partying on the showbiz circuit. Here he looks a little detached from the merriment of Anne Murray, Harry Nilsson, Alice Cooper and Mickey Dolenz.

4 John's hair was big news when cut for the role of Musketeer Gripweed in Richard Lester's unashamedly over the top *How I Won the War* (1967).

1

2

3

4

1

2

Mick Jagger

1 Michael Jagger, athletic mouthpiece of the rebellious Rolling Stones, is the focus of the "world's greatest rock band". His individual style and avante-garde influence made film roles inevitable.
2 With Jean-Luc Godard during the making of *One Plus One* (1968). Razor-sharp Jagger later confessed total ignorance of the film's content.

3 Quick as a flash, society photographer Cecil Beaton clicks with James Fox and Mick on the set of *Performance* (1968).
4 The Wild Colonial Boy makes last minute adjustments on the set of *Ned Kelly* (1970). The movie was based on the adventures of the legendary Australian outlaw and featured Waylon Jennings on the soundtrack.

3

4

Bob Dylan

"I don't want to protest any more. I never said I was an angry young man" – Bob Dylan, August, 1969.

1 Born Robert Allen Zimmerman, Dylan borrowed a name from Mr Thomas and became the darling of the campus liberals and the voice of the majority of minorities.

2 A sideways glance in *Don't Look Back* (1965), D. A. Pennebaker's 16mm *cinéma vérité* masterpiece that was mysteriously withdrawn from distribution in the 1970s.

3 Knock, knock, knocking on Hollywood's door as Alias in Sam Peckinpah's *Pat Garrett and Billy the Kid* (1973), Dylan's only dramatic movie appearance. Peckinpah disowned the film as he didn't edit the final cut.

4 *Renaldo and Clara* (1977), alias Bob and Sara, alias Ronnie and Ronee, took four hours to confuse the critics. A 112 minute version was also made available. Hawkins and Blakley were the two Ronnies.

1

2

3

4

HEAVY PETTING:
The mild ones

"Reeling like a top, snapping his fingers and jerking his eyeballs, with hair like something Medusa had sent back, and a voice that was enormously improved by total unintelligibility." This was John Crosby's description in the *Herald Tribune* of a performance by ace teen idol Fabian.

The teen idol set differed from the original rock 'n' roll stars in many ways. They were certainly more industrious, conquering all areas of show business from concert halls and cabaret, through the pop charts to the small and big screens. Not content with the odd movie cameo role, these mini-Presleys developed into popular screen personalities and tender targets for many an acid critic who couldn't or wouldn't see the talent from the hype.

Charles Eugene Boone, better known to millions as Pat Boone, was the recognized leader of clean-cut-cute teen idols. He was having rock 'n' roll hits as far back as the mid-fifties, although his approach was a million teen miles away from the gyrating raunchiness of a Presley or Lee Lewis. Pat's aim was family appeal and he created his own brand of wholesome rock 'n' roll by covering current black discs in a whiter than white way. Fats Domino's "Ain't That A Shame" and Little Richard's "Tutti Frutti" are prime examples of Boone's output, and for good measure he usually coupled his platters with dreamy young love ballads in the "I'll Be Home" tradition.

With these hit discs behind him and a few TV shows, Pat Boone was signed to a seven year, one picture a year, Twentieth Century-Fox contract for a staggering million dollars and became Elvis Presley's Hollywood neighbour.

Another teen tycoon in the making was Canadian singer/songwriter Paul Anka who moved to Los Angeles and soon established himself in the teen idol stakes. The disc that really catapulted his career into the big-time was the 1957 international best seller "Diana" which he quickly capitalized on with such hits as "You Are My Destiny", "Lonely Boy" and "Puppy Love".

Not surprisingly a movie contract soon came his way and he appeared in a number of films portraying everything from a confused peeping Tom in *Look in Any Window* (1961) to a World War II GI in *The Longest Day* (1962), for which he also supplied the theme song. Keeping him company in *The Longest Day* were Fabian and Tommy Sands.

Tab Hunter's career illustrates this trend in reverse. He had been in movies since his debut in *The Lawless* (1948), and he used his growing screen popularity in the fifties to help send the teen ballad "Young Love" to the top of the pop charts.

The pop charts became a second home for any young actor or actress who showed the slightest musical ability and could hit a right note. The best and most consistent of the breed was Ricky Nelson. Ricky was the son of TV stars Ozzie Nelson and Harriet Hilliard and first appeared as an eight year old on his parents' show, *The Adventures of Ozzie and Harriet*. From that initial episode he was to grow up in full sight of American TV viewers, so that by the time he reached 16 and had cut his first disc, "A Teenager's Romance", there were enough fans beyond the box in TV-land to send it chart-wise.

Another teenage favourite was Johnny Crawford who, between 1957 and 1962, portrayed Chuck Connors' son in the Western series *The Rifleman*. He also used his small screen popularity to secure a number of teen-inspired hits, the biggest being "Cindy's Birthday" and "Rumors" in 1962.

The movie companies recognized the trend. Warner Brothers formed their own record label and released a number of recordings from their stable of young TV stars. Their biggest hit was "Kookie, Kookie, Lend Me Your Comb" which combined the vocal talents of Ed Byrnes, the hip parking lot attendant from *77 Sunset Strip* and Connie Stevens from *Hawaiian Eye*. Byrnes and Stevens also had solo outings with "Like I Love You" and "Sixteen Reasons" respectively, while Roger Smith, co-star of *Sunset Strip*, charted with "Beach Time" and Dorothy Provine from *The Roaring Twenties* Charlestoned her way through "Don't Bring Lulu" and "Crazy Words, Crazy Tune". Other movie and TV companies were also in on the act — Columbia Pictures introduced the Colpix label and Walt Disney Productions founded Buena Vista. Vista recorded, among others, Billy Storm, Hayley Mills, Eddie Hodges, Annette Funicello and the "teenage rave" singer, Tommy Sands.

Sands was a young actor with some stage experience when he was chosen to replace Presley (who had to pull out through pressure of work) in the 1956 TV production *The Singin' Idol*. The role called on him to sing "Teen-age Crush", which he did with such enormous success that by the following year his record version of the song had sold a million copies, earning him a gold disc. Movies and more chart toppers followed in rapid succession.

But when it came to a truly manufactured teen idol production line there was no one to beat the Philadelphia Musak Mafia. This unique family from the City of Brotherly Love included Franklin Avallone (alias Frankie Avalon), Robert Louis Ridarelli (Bobby Rydell), James Ercolani (James Darren), Fabiano Forte (Fabian) and to give their careers that necessary boost — Dick Clark.

Clark's nationally networked rock 'n' pop show *American Bandstand* was beamed direct from Philly into every American teenager's living room. The show's good-time dance party atmosphere, which was interspersed with "Why I'd Like a Date with Sal Mineo"-style competitions, allowed for plenty of guest stars popping in to plug or lip-sync their latest disc (or in the case of Chubby Checker, his latest dance craze). Right on the door step,

Philadelphia's very own Sons of Song were readily available party guests, and soon the names of Avalon, Rydell, Darren and Fabian found their way into every teenager's vocabulary.

Born in 1940, Frankie Avalon was a mere child when he started playing the trumpet and by the time he was twelve years old he had spent a summer season on the Steele Pier, Atlantic City, with the teen band, Rocco and the Saints. Later, after a few TV spots, he returned to Philadelphia and became a regular act at his father's club, a job that lasted until 1956 when the club burnt down. About this time he was introduced to Peter De Angelis and Bob Marcucci who took the then budding vocalist under their wing, signing him to their newly formed Chancellor label.

Avalon once recalled "It seems as though every kid in Philadelphia wanted to be a singer. I was concentrating on my trumpet playing though, until one day I picked up the paper and read about Jimmy Darren. He was right from my neighbourhood and making a career for himself as a singer. I figured that I should be, too." Frankie had very little luck with his first chart attempts, even after performing one of them, "Teacher's Pet", in his first movie, *Disc Jockey Jamboree* (1957). Then came one of those hard-to-believe showbiz quirks of fate. While in the studio cutting "Dede Dinah", as a joke Frankie pinched his nose while singing. The producer loved the effect and, after a massive plug on *American Bandstand*, so did teenage America who sent the disc chartbound. The success brought Hollywood knocking and marked the beginning of Philadelphia's plastic Presley boom.

Soon another ex-member of Rocco and the Saints, Bobby Rydell, followed Frankie Avalon's route to fame and fortune via a Philadelphia record company (this time Cameo Records), *American Bandstand*, a big hit record and a movie contract. Before teenagers had a chance to digest Rydell's sudden rise to stardom, along came a kid who has been described as the "darling of the giggle and scream set" and "the worst pop star the world has known".

Peter De Angelis once recalled: "We were talking to Frankie one day and he said he knew this fifteen-year-old kid at Southern High who looked like a cross between Elvis and Ricky Nelson. So Bob (Marcucci) went over to take a look at the kid. He was so pretty we just knew he had to be a commercial proposition so we signed him up. We taught him a few things vocally, but he never really did go much on singing . . . Anyway, in '58 we did a thing on him called "Lillie Lou" which sold a few around Philadelphia. We were spending quite a lot of money on publicity, getting him known, you know. His next thing was "I'm a Man" and when he did that on *Bandstand* the girls went wild. Then came "Turn Me Loose" and "Tiger" — that sold a million — and we had a monster." The monster was Fabian. Fabian never had much faith in his own ability as a rock singer and soon after the release of his second movie was telling reporters: "It is as an actor that my future lies. After all, pop singers come and go much faster than actors."

Actor James Darren was also spotted while attending Southern High, this time by Hollywood's Joyce Selznick of Screen Gems who signed him to a Columbia Pictures contract. He was soon launched as a lightweight Brando in the *On the Waterfront* inspired *Rumble on the Docks* (1956). He was soon releasing records on Columbia's Colpix label and appearing on *Bandstand* miming to such hits as "Goodbye Cruel World", "Her Royal Majesty" and the title song from the movie *Because They're Young*.

Because They're Young (1960) featured *Bandstand's* Dick Clark as a school teacher in the story based on John Farris's novel *Harrison High*. Directed by Robert Peterson, the film also starred Michael Callan and Tuesday Weld. The nubile Tuesday, who shared the celluloid cheerleader honours with Sandra Dee, Connie Stevens, Annette and Connie Francis, was often quoted in the fanzines about her lovelife. "I steady-date everybody who is fascinating, Dennis Hopper is not my steady", was one of her candid teen-queen quips. Back on the *Because They're Young* soundtrack Bobby Rydell was heard crooning "Swingin' School" while James Darren and Duane Eddy and The Rebels appeared on the screen in cameo roles.

Although based in Phoenix, Arizona, Duane Eddy also had a Philadelphia connection through his record company, Jamie, which had its headquarters in the city, and his regular appearances on *American Bandstand*. On stage Eddy had a moody, laid back appeal, peering over his growling guitar with just a hint of the James Dean little-boy-lost look. He made his acting debut in the TV western series *Have Gun, Will Travel* and struck up a friendship with the show's lead Richard Boone, who was also his co-star in a number of later movies. Never a great actor, Duane Eddy is best remembered for his series of big instrumental hits that include "Movin' 'n' Groovin'", "Rebel Rouser", "Forty Miles of Bad Road", "Because They're Young" and "The Ballad of Paladin", which he recorded as a tribute to the *Have Gun, Will Travel* hero.

James Darren also turned his talents to the small screen, starring in the series *Time Tunnel*. Other television teen heartthrobs who became stars in both the record and the movie worlds included Richard Chamberlain of *Dr Kildare* fame and George Maharis who portrayed Buzz in the excellent road series *Route 66*.

Screened between 1960 and '64, and co-starring Martin Milner as Tod, *Route 66* was based on two free-wheeling buddies who drive their convertible in and out of adventure. The show also boasted such directors as Robert Altman, Richard Donner and Sam Peckinpah and its theme tune became a hit single.

By the mid-sixties the teen kings and queens of the heavy petting league had either engrossed themselves in movie careers, taken to the cabaret circuit, or quietly sunk into a sea of obscurity under the culture shock brought about by the Beatles and the British invasion, while Dick Clark's *American Bandstand* had already moved to the West Coast in time to catch another great teen fad — the Californian surf boom.

2

Pat Boone

1 Portrait of Pat – a boon to parents in the age of the Pelvis.
2 The stall sign says it all. Pat and Shirley Jones in the wholesome *April Love* (1957).
3 Disguised as Casey Jones, James Mason comforts a well-powdered Pat in Henry Levin's *Journey to the Center of the Earth* (1959).
4 Pat Boone plays it close to the chest in *The Perils of Pauline* (1967).

Frankie Avalon

1 Frankie Avalon – a slick package destined for Hollywood.
2 Lumberjack Alan Ladd towers over Frankie in *Guns of the Timberland* (1960).
3 Unperturbed by the weight of a huge raccoon, Frankie Avalon went on to survive John Wayne's *The Alamo* (1960).
4 He was less fortunate in Otto Preminger's *Skidoo* (1969), one of Hollywood's less successful productions.

1

2

3

4

Troy Donahue and **Ed Byrnes**

From the entertainment backlot of the world, Warner Brothers' dream factory produced a range of all-purpose, multi-media teen personalities: the boys, all clean, athletic and well capped; the girls, low-brow blondes with home-town appeal.

The image is best remembered in a host of Delmer Daves movies in which, to the caressing strings of Max Steiner, forever freshman Troy Donahue was let loose to romance every young starlet under contract. These films brought Troy close to: **1** Sandra Dee, junior high's answer to Doris Day, in Sloan Wilson's grand soaper, *A Summer Place* (1959); **2** Connie Stevens, pop singing star of Warner's TV series *Hawaiian Eye*, in *Susan Slade* (1961) and **3** *Parrish* (1961); and **4** Angie Dickinson and Susan Pleshette in *Rome Adventure* (1962). Busy boy Troy also found time for a TV series, *Surfside Six* – not a bad field day and track record for a guy who started life as plain old Merle Johnson.

1

2

3

5 By far the most popular contemporary TV series of the era, *77 Sunset Strip* (1958-62), introduced Warner bit-part actor Ed Byrnes to international recognition and teenage adulation. He owed all his success and fame to the character Kookie – the hair-combin', hot-roddin', jive-talkin', parkin' lot attendant and Dino's Diner employee – a character so strong that when he released (on the WB record label) the novelty record "Kookie Kookie Lend Me Your Comb", aided by Connie Stevens, it became a million seller.

5

4

6

Fabian

1 Old Blue Eyes and Fabian play musical chairs during a break in the filming of *The Hound Dog Man* (1959).

2 How North is West? Fabian with the King of the Cowboys, John Wayne, Stewart Granger and Capucine in Henry Hathaway's slapstick *North to Alaska* (1960).

3 Back to back with Laurie Peters in *Mr Hobbs Takes a Vacation (1962).*

4 Fabian and an original Cindy Doll in *Dear Brigitte* (1956).

5 Hard-driving Fabian in *Thunder Alley* (1967).

1

2

3

4

5

Annette Funicello

1 Annette "I have had countless thrills" Funicello eventually escaped the Mickey Mouse trap at Walt Disney Productions, partly because of her burgeoning voluptuousness.
2 Annette shows a dimpled thigh during a break with Bobbi Shaw on the set of *Pajama Party* (1964), an AIP beach movie.
3 Annette, Fabian and Frankie, the Italian set, in *Fireball 500* (1966).

She was the queen of Hollywood's junior ratpack. She was there to welcome Presley home from the army, and she was at her bitchin' best with "These Boots are made for Walking" she's . . . **Nancy Sinatra.**
4 An off-camera cuddle for Nancy Sinatra from husband Tommy Sands during the shooting of *For Those Who Think Young* (1964).
5 Nancy well tied up with Peter Fonda for *The Wild Angels* (1966).

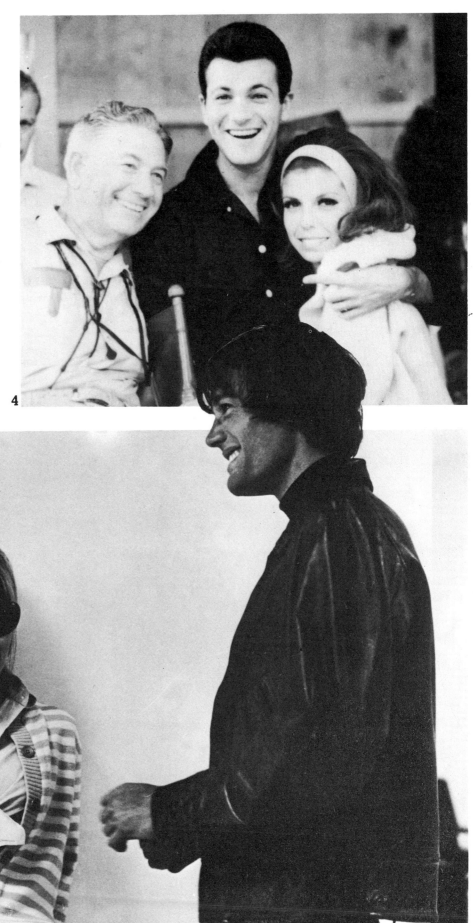

4

5

Tuesday Weld

1 Thirteen years old and strapless, Tuesday Weld hits the screen with the singing voice of Connie Francis in *Rock, Rock, Rock* (1957).

2 At the Harrison High sock-hop it's back to the wall for Tuesday as Michael Callan closes in *Because They're Young* (1960).

3 36-19-35 and seventeen years old. Susan Weld proclaims "I'm an actress, a very fine actress and I do not want to be known as a model". This view was supported by Twentieth Century-Fox who said "She is a combination of Garbo, Brando, Monroe, Lanza, plus a little of Shirley Temple, Diane Varsi, and . . . looking from the rear like Jayne Mansfield's kid sister."

Connie Francis

Apart from having been the singing voices of both Tuesday Weld and Jayne Mansfield, Connie Francis also found her own movie roles.

4 *Where the Boys Are* (1960) – Paula Prentiss, Dolores Hart, Yvette Mimieux and, making her debut, the statuesque Connie at a Fort Lauderdale location. Based on the book by Glen Swarthout, the story followed four college girls and their first adventure away from home. For a teen movine M.G.M. gave it a huge budget of $3,000,000.

5 Dressed entirely in an illuminated manuscript, Cinderella awaits Prince Charming in *Follow the Boys* (1963).

6 Connie has tooth trouble but still has more bite than *Looking for Love* (1964).

1

2

3

4

5

6

Ricky Nelson

1 Ricky Nelson made his film debut with horse opera veterans John Wayne, Ward Bond and Walter Brennan in Howard Hawks' classic *Rio Bravo* (1959).

2 "What am I bid for this wooden replica of Ricky Nelson" asks Jack Lemmon in *The Wackiest Ship in the Army* (1961), an original blend of comedy and wartime suspense directed by Richard Murphy.

Richard Chamberlain

3 A new high in dedicated sincerity was brought to the small screen by Richard Chamberlain as Doctor Kildare. He was also to take the TV show's theme song to the top of the pop charts.

Tab Hunter

4 Art Gelien, better known as Tab Hunter, shows commendable calmness in the face of the marine fungus that is attacking his legs in *Saturday Island* (1952).

5 Cheek to cheek – Tab with Debbie Reynolds in the Fred Astaire vehicle *The Pleasure of His Company* (1961).

3

5

4

1

2

3

Tommy Sands

1 The gospel according to Tommy Sands, as he struggles to survive the pressures of religion and rock 'n' roll stardom in *Sing, Boy, Sing* (1958).
2 The reviews could have been better for *Babes in Toyland* (1961), even with the pouting presence of Annette Funicello.
3 *Love in a Goldfish Bowl* (1961) left the critics open-mouthed at its sheer banality. A blond Tommy Sands cleans up around co-stars Fabian and Toby Michaels.

Bobby Rydell

4 Jessie Pearson as Conrad Birdie sees stars as Bobby Rydell swings into a film career that never got off the canvas – *Bye Bye Birdie* (1963) and bye bye Bobby.

George Chakiris

5 George Chakiris lost for words in the face of plaid-panted Jackie Lane in *Two and Two Makes Six* (1961).
6 He fared much better as Bernardo in the Academy Award winning *West Side Story* (1961) in which Shakespeare and juvenile delinquency were set against a New York skyline.

Chubby Checker

1 A life of parallels lay ahead for Ernie Evans, a Philly slaughterman. It started when Dick Clark's wife, fan of Fats Domino, rechristened him Chubby Checker. It was then but a dance step away from *Rock Around the Clock* to *Twist Around the Clock* (1961) and from **2** *Don't Knock the Rock* to *Don't Knock the Twist* (1962).

Duane Eddy

3 "Who twanged?" asks Dick Boone. Duane Eddy's guilty look gives him away in *A Thunder of Drums* (1961).

Hayley Mills

1 Hayley Mills, a caged kitten in J. Lee Thompson's Cardiff-based drama *Tiger Bay* (1959).
2 Hayley caused double trouble for Maureen O'Hara and Brian Keith in *The Parent Trap* (1961). This movie produced her smash hit "Let's Get Together".
3 The bells were ringing for Hywel Bennett and his girl in *The Family Way* (1967), the movie adapted from Bill Naughton's TV play *All in Good Time* and notable for a fleeting glimpse of a Mills posterior as well as a soundtrack by Paul McCartney.

1

3

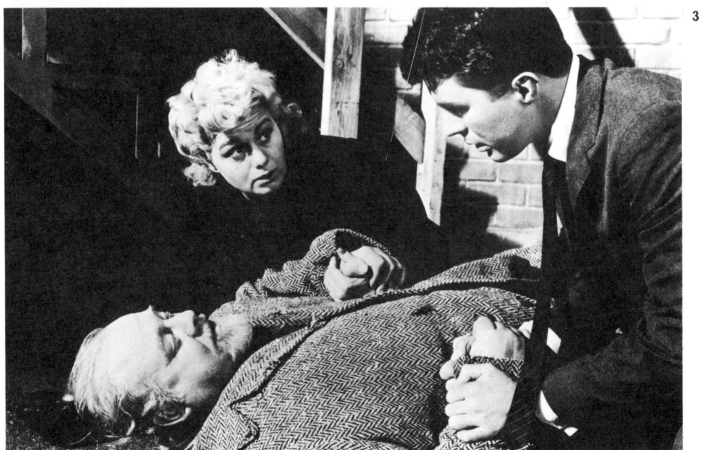

2

James Darren

1 A racketeer in a Raymond Burr
hand-me-down pals up with James
Darren who finds support in the
shape of Robert Blake. *Rumble on
the Docks* (1966), directed by Fred F.
Sears, was a wimp's *On the
Waterfront.*
2 Cold hands and warm hearts for
Jean Seberg and Jimmy in *Let No
Man Write My Epitaph* (1960).
3 Directed by Philip Leacock, the
film also featured heavyweights
Shelley Winters and Burl Ives – who
could have swallowed a fly, we don't
know why, perhaps he died.
4 Yvette Mimieux puts on a bold
front as Darren's hands start to
wander in *Diamond Head* (1962).

4

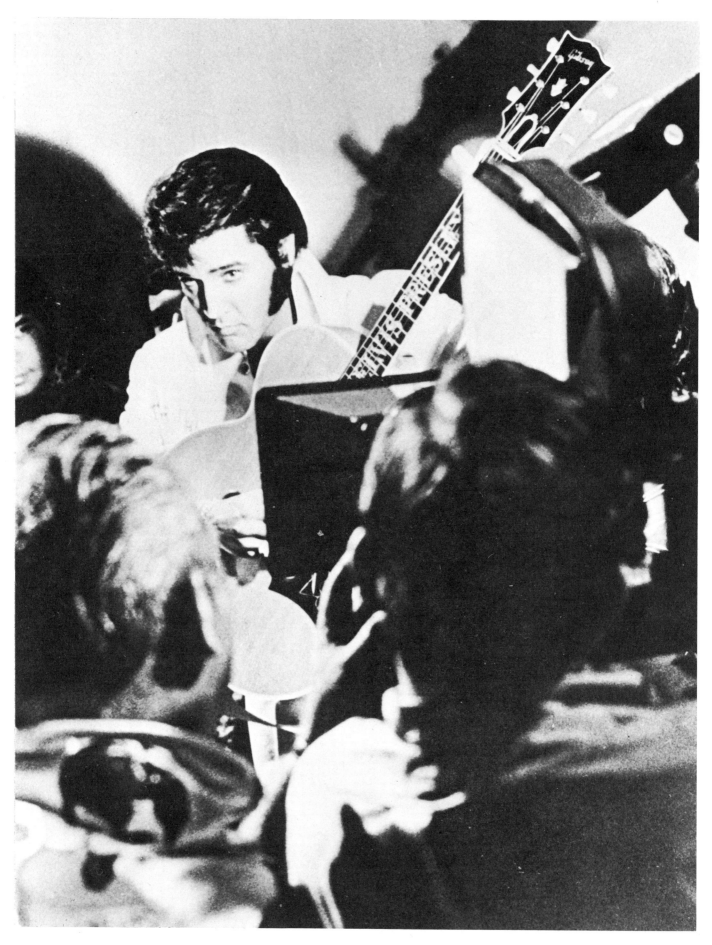

PRESLEY:
Filming star

Elvis Presley was the acknowledged King of Rock 'n' Roll. He dominated the rock scene of the fifties as he "outsold, outfilmed, out-rocked and outraged" everyone. His ability to pull them in to the cinemas, no matter how awful the film, was unfortunately exploited during the sixties, but his unique magnetism re-emerged at the end and he died, still the King.

Elvis

1 Presley's introductory vehicle was *Love Me Tender* (1956), produced by Hollywood veteran Hall Wallis, seen emerging from the sound stages with Elvis.

2 Originally entitled *The Reno Brothers,* Wallis changed the name of the film when he heard the star's rendition of "Love Me Tender". A very shrewd move as it turned out – the song went straight to the top of the charts and the movie made cinema history by recouping its entire production cost in the first three days of release.

Playing a confused kid caught up in the Civil War, Presley manages four songs before getting shot, but reappears at the end in ghostly form. The film was one of his best, partly because he was able to portray aspects of his own character. However, some reviewers were less than enthusiastic: "Thick-lipped, droopy-eyed, and indefatigably sullen, Mr Presley, whose talents are meagre but whose earnings are gross, excites a large section of the young female population as nobody else has ever done, and I approached the movie with a certain amount of middle-aged trepidation. Unhappily, my fears were well founded" – John McCarten, *New Yorker.*

3 Such criticism never dampened the aspiration of Presley's doting mother, Gladys, pictured having fun with her golden boy on the set.

4 And besides, Elvis and his good-ol'-boy entourage could always hold their own with the press.

1

1

3

1 A grave confrontation between Deke Rivers (Elvis) and Glenda Markle (Lizabeth Scott) in the well-received *Loving You* (1957), directed by Hal Kanter.

2 Widely considered to be the pinnacle of rock choreography, Elvis leads his cell mates through the title number of *Jailhouse Rock* (1957).

3 Directed by Richard Thorpe, the movie starred the late Judy Tyler as Peggy Van Alden and Elvis as Vince Everett. Here Peggy listens to the famous Presley pout.

4 Elvis as a delinquent Quasimodo stands his ground against switchblader Vic Morrow in *King Creole* (1958). Based on Harold Robbins' *A Stone for Danny Fisher* and directed by veteran Michael Curtiz *King Creole* has stood the test of time and is considered by many to be the archetypal Presley vehicle.

4

1 No sooner out of fatigues than back in again for *GI Blues* (1960) and the start of his post-army career. Juliet Prowse as Lili partners Tulsa McLean for a camp dance.

2 Elvis waits for his crew mates to fix the tank as these were not the tracks he was used to laying down.

3 Originally conceived as a Marlon Brando vehicle, *Flaming Star* (1960) provided Elvis with the opportunity to show what he could do given the right script and the right director, in this case Don Siegel. Unfortunately, subsequent projects failed to supply these ingredients.

4 A close encounter for Glen and Noreen (Tuesday Weld) in *Wild in the Country* (1961), directed by Philip Dunne and co-starring Hope Lange, Millie Perkins and John Ireland.

1

2

1 Palm trees, pineapples and pretty girls surround beachboy Elvis in *Blue Hawaii* (1961). As Chad, Elvis polly-wolly-doodles his way through "Rock-a-Hula Baby".
2 Elvis blends in as one of the boys in a Honolulu hoe-down.
3 Colonel Tom surrenders the name of his tailor while on the set of *Follow That Dream* (1962).
4 In *Follow That Dream* Elvis drifts his way through the first of those all too familiar Presley packages.

3

4

1 In the title role of *Kid Galahad* (1962) Elvis did his best to pack a punch, but even the presence of Gig Young and Charles Bronson failed to make the movie more than "a dismal remake of the 1937 classic".

2 Elvis as Ross Carpenter trips the light fantastic with Laurel Dodge (Laurel Goodwin) in Norman Taurog's *Girls! Girls! Girls!* (1962).

3 *It Happened at the World's Fair*, or did it? Judging by this thrusting uninhibited encounter between Yvonne Craig and Big E it seems unlikely.
4 In a dramatic cockpit scenario, Elvis' barnstorming enthusiasm for flying was vividly portrayed.

1

2

3

78

1 Elvis plummets to new heights of depth in *Fun in Acapulco* (1963). The film is notable for the appearance of Ursula Andress, fresh from her sensational bikini clad role in *Dr No* (1963).

2 Lucky Jackson (Elvis) is faced with one of Rusty Martin's (Ann-Margaret) big .45s in *Viva Las Vegas* (1964).

3 In *Kissin' Cousins* (1964) Pamela Austin and Yvonne Craig pull an Elvis each in this dual-role Presley vehicle.

4 *Roustabout* (1964) gives Elvis a chance to shine as Charlie Rogers, a free-wheeling, singing karate expert.

1 Gary Crosby (left) joins Elvis in *Girl Happy* (1965). In it Presley breaks new ground by appearing in drag.

2 In *Tickle Me* (1965) we were once again privileged to watch Presley be sad, then happy again, then sad again, in a stunning display of emotional pyrotechnics.

3 In this dramatic scene from *Harum Scarum* (1965) one of the least wooden performances was put in by a large post.

4 "Scriptless, directionless and virtually tuneless" summed up *Frankie and Johnny* (1966).

4

1 Out of work aviator Rick Richards (Elvis) gasps in astonishment when he discovers exactly how complicated the twiddly bit at the pointed end is, in Michael Moore's *Paradise, Hawaiian Style* (1966).
2 Elvis as Mike McCoy makes a discreet entrance in an LA nitespot for Norman Taurog's *Spinout* (1966). This film included the memorable song "Smorgasbord". Smorgas was not the only one.

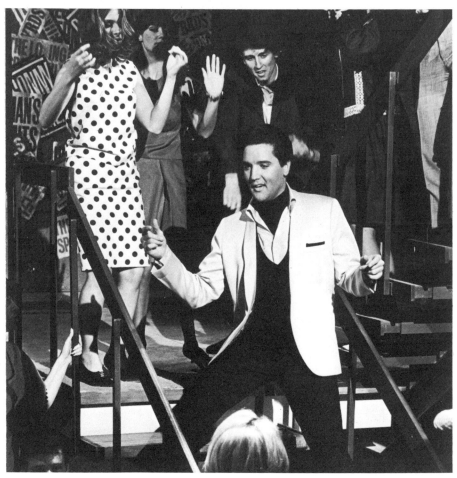

3 Frogman Ted Jackson (Elvis) pulls the plug on Jo Symington (Dodie Marshall). His relaxed style of motoring appears to have unhinged his hapless passenger(s) in *Easy Come, Easy Go* (1967).

4 Jill Conway (Annette Day) steadies an Elvis reeling from the shock of finding himself in a film which has lines and things. The critics were surprised enough to make comment on *Double Trouble* (1967).

5 Scott Hayward (Elvis) thanks the waitress for mending his jacket in a scene from *Clambake* (1967). Will Hutchins wishes he was back on the set of *Sugarfoot*.

1 *Speedway* (1968) was only remarkable in that it was the first Elvis movie to be released as a B feature in Great Britain. Even IRS inspector Nancy Sinatra was unable to rescue the film.

2 Into the downward slide. Symbolically, in *Stay Away Joe* (1968) Elvis, as Joe Lightcloud, gets his money by selling off his car piece by piece. Presley seemed to be doing the same with his career and distributors in the UK wouldn't release the film.

3 It was the same story for *Live a Little, Love a Little* (1968) which, as Albert the Great Dane will testify, was a dog of a movie.

4 Originally entitled *Have Girls, Will Travel*, *The Trouble with Girls (and How to Get Into It)* (1969) did little to revive the audiences' interest.

1

2

3

4

3

4

1 In the role of saddle tramp Jess Wade in *Charro* (1969), Elvis came closer than he had for a long time to achieving the promise first shown in *Flaming Star*.

2 Dr John Carpenter (Elvis) prays that Sister Michelle (Mary Tyler Moore) is not really a nun – kitchen sink drama Presley-style in *Change of Habit* (1969).

3 Something of the former Presley stepped from the shadows in *Elvis – That's the Way It Is* (1970), a happy and welcome departure from the long series of Hollywood formula films.

4 It was backed up by *Elvis on Tour* (1972) in which The King returned to do what he had always done best. Compiled from a sensational 15 concert tour, and including a film montage of earlier material edited by Martin Scorsese, this last appearance on film recaptures much of the unique magnetism and power that gave rise to a legend.

BRITISH ROCK:
The Empire strikes back

Jiving at the church hall to the local tea-chest and washboard brigade; snapping garters in the back row of the flicks; doing a ton on a Beezer; chatting up birds in the coffee bar, while lingering over a frothy coffee and listening to one of the many emerging home-grown Presleys — this was the scene in pre-Beatle Britain. Lacking the glitter and style of their American counterparts, Britain's first rock singers reflected the parochialism and austerity of the post-war period.

Britain's first real answer to Elvis was the Bermondsey merchant seaman, Tommy Hicks, who every time the boat came in would trundle his guitar down to the 2 Is coffee bar in London's Soho to perform his music. Mid-way through a set he was spotted by what used to be called a "talent scout" and a recording contract with Decca Records was quickly presented. His name was changed to Tommy Steele. Such descriptive surnames became a fad among British rock 'n' roll singers — Billy Fury, Adam Faith, Marty Wilde, Duffy Power, Johnny Gentle and Vince Eager were to follow. With his new name and group, the Steelmen, Decca released "Rock with the Cave Man". Three hits later he was starring in his own biopic, *The Tommy Steele Story* (1957). A later movie, *Expresso Bongo* (1959), was also based on Tommy's meteoric rise to stardom, but this time the central character was played by another young coffee bar cowboy, Cliff Richard.

Cliff Richard (alias Harry Webb) followed Steele as contender in British Presley stakes. He certainly looked the part and he could curl his lip, an image producer Jack Good was looking for to headline his new TV rock 'n' roll show *Oh Boy!*. Cliff became a resident on the show and after a handful of UK hits made his movie debut in *Serious Charge* (1959). The film produced his biggest hit "Living Doll", a song Cliff had been reported as not particularly caring for. Although the record made an impression on the US charts, Cliff and his group the Shadows (who had become famous in their own right as top instrumentalists) eventually settled down to a comfortable pedestrian pop movie career in a series of "Hey Fellas, let's do the show right here" vehicles, augmented by regular hits, concert tours and TV appearances.

Billy Fury and Adam Faith were hot on Cliff's heels as England's top teenage heartthrobs. Liverpool-born Billy (Ronald Wincherley) came from impresario Larry Parnes' young stable of rock hopefuls and was the closest the UK came to producing a true rockabilly stylist in the early Elvis tradition. In fact he became the centre of so much criticism aimed at his below-the-belt stage act, that he was forced to change direction, or at least switch emphasis. Fury announced he was "cleaning up" the act and turning to middle-of-the-road movies and disc ballads, he achieved his ambition.

Adam Faith was born Terence Nelhams in Acton, London. After serving his pop apprenticeship performing on the coffee bar circuit, followed by some unspectacular discs and TV appearances, he was chosen (thanks to an introduction by John Barry) as resident singer on the TV rock show *Drumbeat*. The show produced that necessary shot in the arm his career badly needed and within months he was given his movie break in *Beat Girl* (1960) while also riding high in the pop charts. Faith's image (like that of Jet Harris) owed more to James Dean than Presley and he later became the real actor of the original bunch.

Other early British rockers who achieved varying degrees of movie success included Marty Wilde, Joe Brown and Jess Conrad. Conrad appeared in the first of two UK youth movies to feature pre-swinging England teenagers with some sense of realism.

The Boys (1962) directed by Sidney J. Furie, was a courtroom drama about four youths who, after a seemingly aimless but innocent night on the town, are charged with robbery and murder. Helping the action along, the soundtrack featured the Shadows in attuned sympathetic form.

The second movie, *Some People* (1962), had its premiere at the Plaza, London attended by none other than the Duke of Edinburgh. The reason behind his patronage becomes clear when you realize that the plot revolved around teenage boredom and the alternatives offered by the Duke's Awards Scheme. Within what could have been simply a do-gooding exercise, director Clive Donner injected some choice teen culture and a bit of historic insight. The opening motorcycle scenes were suitably realized and fashioned with just the right amount of black leather jacket and white silk scarf. Angela Wilkes provided an unforgettable bath scene in which she shrank her brand new jeans while still in them. What really made the movie a classic piece of teen culture lay partly in its Bristol location, but more importantly because its young working class hero, Ray Brooks, lived on a council estate, played the guitar and had musical ambitions — a perfect reflection of what was really happening in every provincial city across the UK, that climaxed a year later in Mersey Mania.

Although the British pre-Beatle stars and movies found enthusiastic home audiences, sadly it was clear that they did not travel well. This point was highlighted as recently as 1976 when the prestigious US *Rolling Stone* magazine published their *Illustrated History of Rock and Roll*; within its well researched covers lay a photo of Joe Brown and Billy Fury flanked by Gene Vincent and Eddie Cochran with a caption that informs the readers Joe is Tommy Steele and Billy a mere fan.

Tommy Steele

1 Tommy buys a four string guitar, which is still three more strings than he needs, in another forgettable scene from *The Tommy Steele Story* (1957).

2 Tuxedoed and tidy, Tommy triumphant in *The Duke Wore Jeans* (1958), a double identity caper in which he played the duke and the jeans.

3 Benny Hill and Tommy Steele as fraternal hoofers from a searchlight battery in *Light Up the Sky* (1959).

4 Janet Munro twiddles Tommy's tassel in the facile yet successful *Tommy the Toreador* (1960), a movie immortalized by the hit song apparently entitled "Lil Whoi Boow" but strangely credited as "Little White Bull".

1

2

3

Billy Fury

Billy Fury could have been one of the biggest . . . he certainly had the looks, the talent and a voice. Sadly, ill-health dogged him throughout his career, forcing him to take time out, until finally he died of a heart attack at the start of what many pundits believe would have been a major comeback.

1 For Shane Fenton's eyes only: Billy Fury demonstrates his twista-billi-ty as Billy Universe.

2 Billy never got past the post and disappointed the punters in his second film, *I've Got a Horse* (1965).

1

2

Adam Faith

1 Already an established pop star, Adam Faith was on home ground as a tearaway teenager of the expresso set in *Beat Girl* (1960).
2 Adam had difficulty getting his leg over for John Guillermine's *Never Let Go* (1961), a film notable for Peter Sellers' one and only sadistic screen role.
3 Hunched on an icy street location during the shooting of *Mix Me a Person* (1962), Adam receives direction from Leslie Norman for his role as a wrongly accused garage mechanic.

Cliff Richard

1 Rocking at the youth club: Cliff hits a high note on the million dollar set of *Serious Charge* (1959). This controversial small town drama, directed by Terence Young, gave Cliff his first big international hit, "Living Doll".

2 Dental dazzler Bongo Herbert (Cliff Richard) attracts admiring glances from an excited matelot and assorted onlookers in the finger-snapping hit *Expresso Bongo* (1959).

3 Carefree Cliff on a busman's holiday to sunshine and romance takes time out to walk the dog with lovely Laurie Peters in tow while making the armchair travelogue *Summer Holiday* (1963).

1

2

3

4

Terry Dene

4 Sugary smiles all round as a macho Terry Dene thanks his backers with a soppy song from *Golden Disc* (1958).

Helen Shapiro

5 Husky Helen Shapiro clutches a bent straw, a dreamy smile playing on the perfectly formed lips of Golders Green's answer to Paul Robeson, from Richard Lester's hectic, zany *It's Trad, Dad!* (1962).

5

Marty Wilde and Joe Brown

Marty Wilde and Joe Brown have over the years become crepe-soled pillars of England's rock 'n' roll hierarchy. Wilde (father of the nubile Kim) is the man most likely to be called upon to comment on the passing of a fellow contemporary, while jumpin' Joe (who doesn't look a day older than when he was topping the charts with "A Picture of You") often pops up on tele commercials promoting yet another great twenty vintage tracks culled from the archives.

1 Would-be pop idols Marty Wilde and Joe Brown look as if they can't afford the ticket to stardom in *It's a Crazy World* (1963).

2 In an attempt to develop his stature, Marty Wilde tried his hand at acting in *The Hellions* (1968). Directed by Ken Annakin, the movie was a pure Western revenge opus transported to 19th century South Africa.

3 The Cockney with the coconut hairdo, chirpy Joe Brown wallops it to them in *Just For Fun* (1963), which featured a musical cast of thousands.

1

2

3

All the fun of the fair. Julie Harris and
James Dean are all hands in *East of
Eden* (1954).

JAMES DEAN

... the bad boy from a good family

WARNER BROS.' CHALLE

OF TODAY'S TEENAGE VIO

also starring **NATALIE WOOD** with SAL MINEO

JIM BACKUS · ANN DORAN · COREY ALLEN · WILLIAM HOPPER

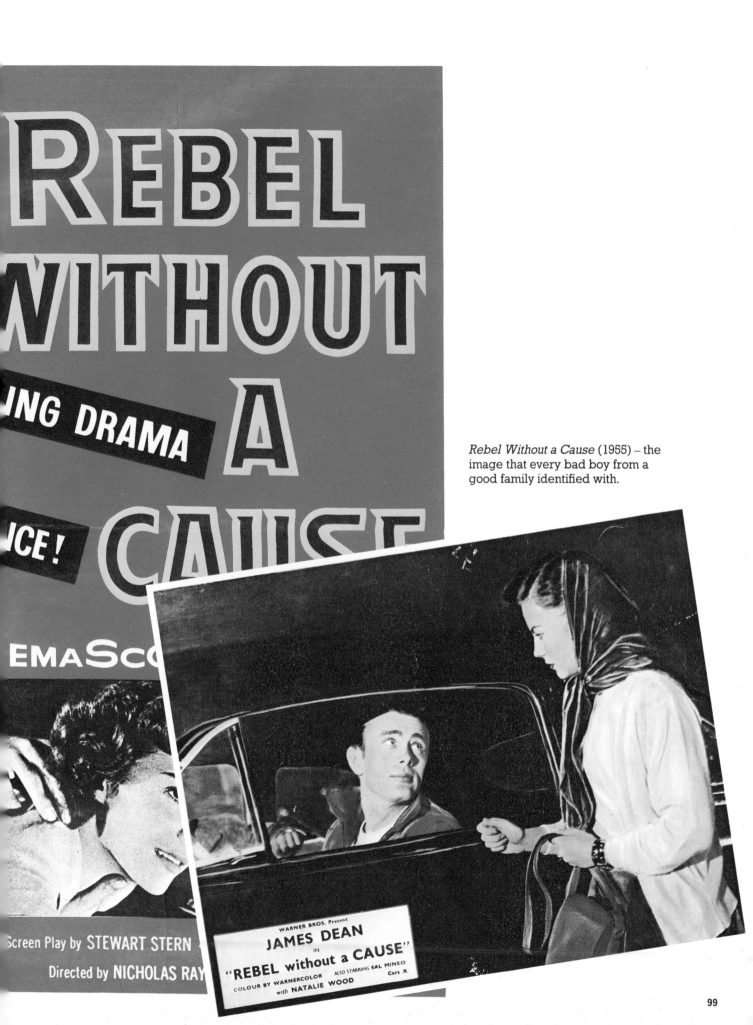

Rebel Without a Cause (1955) – the image that every bad boy from a good family identified with.

"Hi, this is Elvis Presley. I guess the first thing that people want to know is why I can't stand still when I'm singing. Some people tap their feet, some people snap their fingers and some people just sway back and forth. I just started doing them all together, I guess."

"I watch my audiences and I listen to them and I know that we're all getting something out of our system, but none of us knows what is is. The important thing is that we're getting rid of it and nobody's getting hurt." Elvis with an early message to fans.

1 "When the years have flown" – Cliff, Carole Gray and Ruislip Lido from *The Young Ones* (1961).

2 Bruce, Brian, Liquorice and Hank casting shadows in *Summer Holiday* (1963).

1

1 Beachniks Sandra Dee, James Darren and Cliff Robertson discuss the varied pleasures of riding waves in the archetypal beach movie *Gidget* (1959).

2 Most surf music acts were quick to jump aboard Hollywood's celluloid woodie. Beach Boy Mike aids the queen of the beach bunnies, Annette Funicello, in what the official caption described as "The Wild Watusi title song" from *The Monkey's Uncle* (1965).

3 This winning formula climaxed with Don Taylor's big beach opus, *Ride the Wild Surf* (1964). Surf music's dynamic duo Jan and Dean who gained chart success with the title song were also to co-star, but as Dean Torrance once remembered: "Jan and I were supposed to be in this epic – our film debut co-starring Fabian. But right about the same time a close friend kidnapped Frank Sinatra Jr., so the movie people kicked me out of the film. I think they thought that another one of my friends might try to kidnap Fabian."

2

3

'Help! (1965), the Beatles' second feature film (and first in colour), turned out to be slicker, glossier and more surreal than its predecessor. Although very much of the era, the movie manages to stand the test of time and has even been nominated "Best Rock Movie" by the king of the B feature, Roger Corman.

1 The Bahamas Cycle Club on the road.

2 A portrait of John, rock's departed and sadly missed prince.

3 George Harrison the dime store guru in tie-and-dyes.

1

1 James Marshall Hendrix caught at
the climax of his fluid set at
Monterey, from *Monterey Pop* (1969).
Tragically Jimi died through drug
abuse in September 1970.
2 Only a month later fellow
Monterey performer Janis Joplin
suffered the same fate.

2

1

2

1 Dusky Diana Ross in her movie debut, *Lady Sings the Blues* (1972). Although Diana gave a good account of herself, and even won an Academy Award nomination, most critics felt it was a highly inaccurate biopic of jazz singer Billie Holiday.

2 Daria (where are you now?) Halprin, the happy hippie, in Antonioni's cultist *Zabriskie Point* (1970), aptly named as nobody got it.

3 Bowie bites his lip as Candy Clark gives her all, in one hugely reassuring glance, in Nicholas Roeg's sci-fi movie, *The Man Who Fell to Earth* (1976).

3

1 *American Graffiti* (1973) – "A neon drive-in casts long shadows across a vast parking lot as the sun drops behind a distant hill. A large neon sign buzzes in the foreground . . . MELS DRIVE-IN, while in the background 'Rock Around the Clock' blares from the radio of a beautiful decked and channeled, white with red trim, tuck-and-rolled '58 Chevy Impala that glides into the drive-in. Main titles appear over action . . ." and that's just the beginning . . .

2 British graffiti – Ringo Starr (Mike) clocks the golf while David Essex (Jim) looks like he's just lost another threepenny bit in *That'll Be the Day* (1973).

3 The cast rallies round for yet another fish-that-broke-the-line story from the Fonz in TV's *Happy Days*. This popular series owed much of its endearing innocence and charm to the influence of *American Graffiti*.

Where w

American

It was the time of making it with the birds, doin' the Twist and all that Jive. It was the time of your life.

· Starring RICHARD DREY
ORIA KATZ & WILLARD H
ISTRIBUTED BY CINEMA

2

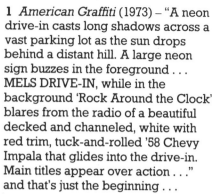

Paul McCartney carrying the weight
of *Let It Be* (1970).

John Leyton

John Leyton built a strong teenage following playing Ginger in the ATV television series *Biggles*. But, it wasn't until the success of his later TV role as Johnny St Cyr in the popular *Harper West One* series that he launched himself into the pop world. Under the musical auspices of the legendary producer Joe Meek, John charted with the two mini pop classics "Johnny Remember Me" and "Wild Wind" while continuing to pursue his big screen career.

He went underground for **4** *The Great Escape* (1963), **5** surfaced (but still behind the wire) in a British holiday camp in *Every Day's a Holiday* (1964), and **6** went back underground, looking for a way out, in *Von Ryan's Express* (1965).

4

5

6

Jess Conrad

1 A seminal figure in modern music and drama, London-born Gerald James (Jess Conrad) rocked a whole generation to sleep. Three of his golden greats were selected for a compilation album of the world's 30 worst songs, a feat that has yet to be equalled.

2 Elizabeth (Pauline Hahn), a dangerous delinquent, is shown the path to redemption by Peter, maturely portrayed by Jess in Muriel Box's *Too Young to Love* (1959).

3 Jess is severely abused by a mutant chimp while cruising on his Vespa in *Konga* (1961).

4

4 Jess's virtuoso plucking goads Elizabeth Shepherd into a flamenco frenzy in this confused scene from the "museum piece" *The Queen's Guards* (1961).
5 Dudley Sutton, Ronald Lacey, Tony Garnett and Jess during their night on the town that ultimately led to accusations of murder and a powerful courtroom drama in Sidney J. Furie's *The Boys* (1962).

5

1

2

Ray Brooks

Ray Brooks caught the mood of the times and the changing UK scene in a couple of fine movies. However, his real *tour de force* came in the role of Carol White's luckless husband in the award-winning BBC TV series *Cathy Come Home*.

1 Apparently unable to play their own instruments, Ray Brooks, David Hemmings and David Andrews as a local beat group mimed convincingly to a sound track provided by Valerie Mountain and The Eagles in *Some People* (1962). Like so many young hopefuls who stood at windy bus stops, they missed the bus.
2 After *A Hard Day's Night* Richard Lester gave us *The Knack* (1965), as demonstrated by Ray Brooks, which signalled the arrival of Swingin' London.

The second great world rock and teen explosion happened in the early sixties and originated in England. Nobody was more pleasantly surprised than the British to learn that suddenly they were pace and trendsetters. Spearheaded by the Beatles, the English beat-wave crossed the Atlantic, opening Pandora's box in the biggest take-over pop had known. Using the Beatles as brand leaders, *Life* magazine later summed up this fabulous phenomenon "Borrowing the basics from American rock, then putting it through the filter of their Liverpool background, the four Beatles came up with a sound — and a manner — that ran away with the early sixties."

Before teenage girls across the globe had a chance to take the first wave of cuddly mop-tops to their collective breast, along came a second wave who were even more fab, more gear and more mod. Also in the running were the Dave Clark Five, Gerry and the Pacemakers, the Searchers, Peter and Gordon, the Animals and the Rolling Stones, all contributing to a new highly creative Elizabethan age. Soon important American magazines sent photographers over and coined phrases like "Swingin' London" and the world heard of a Soho backstreet that rightfully claimed to be the world's fashion centre, while a damp Liverpool cellar club was humming as the hive of rock-culture.

Emanating from the northern seaport's Cavern Club, the Mersey beat groups, closely followed by others, from Manchester to Tottenham, sent a teenage shock wave around the world and it wasn't long before they brought a new lease of life to an already faltering British film industry. They churned out movie after movie as if celluloid was going out of fashion: Gerry and the Pacemakers' *Ferry Cross the Mersey* (1964), Dave Clark's *Catch Us If You Can* (1964), the Searchers' *Saturday Night Out* (1964) and the exploitive package *Just For You* (1964) were only a few of the pop out-takes.

Running parallel with the interest in all things English created by the beat boys, Britain's new breed of screen actors — headed by the young rebel of *Saturday Night and Sunday Morning* (1960) and *Tom Jones* (1963), Albert Finney, the comic genius of Peter Sellers and the *enfant gâté* Hayley Mills — quickly gained international superstar status. Those who also struck the rich vein included Sean '007' Connery, Michael Caine, Susannah York, Terence Stamp, Julie Christie, David Hemmings, Rita Tushingham, Alan Bates, Sarah Miles, James Fox, Hywel Bennett, Oliver Reed, Lynn and Vanessa Redgrave, Michael York and Tom Courtnay; while a couple of England's and the sixties' best known clothespegs, Jean Shrimpton and Twiggy, also found big screen success.

The young and lovely Hayley Mills had been rediscovered by Walt Disney after viewing the British crime thriller *Tiger Bay* (1959), and she was soon under contract and in Hollywood making *Pollyanna* (1960) quickly followed by *The Parent Trap* (1961). *The Parent Trap* (originally titled *Petticoats and Blue Jeans*) called for her not only to portray twins Sue and Sharon but to sing "Let's Get Together" in over-dubbed harmony. This on screen and record success gave her US teen star status — in the heavy petting class. By the mid-sixties Hayley had developed into a fine actress, helped by her first husband and mentor Roy Boulting, who starred her in a string of highly accomplished movies such as *The Family Way* (1967) and *Twisted Nerve* (1969).

Others that prospered during the British onslaught included Scots actor David McCallum who became a teen hero as Ilya Kuryakin in the TV secret agent series *The Man from Uncle*, a show so popular it spawned the spin-off *The Girl from Uncle* featuring another UK exile, Noel Harrison. Both Harrison and McCallum used this television popularity in individual attempts at the pop charts, with Harrison coming off fractionally better. However, McCallum did milk the role further with a couple of full length movies based on the series that fitted in nicely with the popular spy genre of the day. Not only the actors, but the whole British film industry rose to the bait. For probably the first time in their history UK film makers didn't have to rely on American star names and exotic locations to sell their movies abroad . . . all they needed was right there, at home in their own backyards.

London swung-on in a series of movies capturing its time and place. *Alfie* (1966) stands out as a good example, with Michael Caine in the title role of the amorous Cockney whose life style seemed to be in line with the new found permissiveness. He said, "I think if you were to spend all your time with birds you'd begin to feel you're going a bit doolally. It's my opinion there isn't one in a thousand right in the head, but I must admit I love 'em. I mean they give a bloke so much pleasure in his life" — a bit of rhetoric that clearly summed-up his philosophy. In one stylish sense *Alfie* carried on from where *Tom Jones* (1963) left off, for in many key scenes Caine turned to the audience and talked in a frank and sometimes intimate way. The movie was a huge success and made Michael Caine an international star. It was certainly enjoyed by one Burt Bacharach who after viewing the film rushed home and quickly knocked off "What's It All About?".

Blow-up (1967), directed by Antonioni, very definitely caught the decadence of the period, with David Hemmings as a trendy London photographer who, while viewfinding, believes he has witnessed a murder. This sometimes baffling movie also included an appearance by the Yardbirds and an erotic scene with Jane Birkin.

Except for a handful of concert movies and Jean-Luc Godard's *One Plus One* (1969), where they are seen in the studio recording "Sympathy for the Devil", the Rolling Stones, unlike their singer Mick Jagger, never really took the movie initiative. Mick certainly looked at home in front of the cameras, appearing in a couple of movies with some critical and artistic success. But even before production had started on Jagger's best movie, *Performance* (1968), a new movement had emerged from a new youth-culture capital. The San Francisco hippies introduced new ways of expression through their drop-out culture of sex, drugs and rock 'n' roll.

1

2

1 Fighting fit former stuntman Dave Clark drags Barbara Ferris and Tottenham's answer to the Beatles behind him in that endless sprint *Catch Us If You Can* (1965).
2 A close second in the athletics stakes came the Hermits, trailed by their pained leader, Herman, in *Mrs. Brown, You've Got a Lovely Daughter* (1968).

1 Gerry and the Pacemakers take their turn on stage at the Cavern in *Ferry Cross the Mersey* (1965). Sadly this hallowed hall of the Mersey Sound was later demolished, an event that roughly coincided with the demise of the Pacemakers.

2 Riding on the Mersey boom, ex-Cavern hat check girl Cilla Black wore a nice hat and gloves to play opposite David Warner in *Work Is a Four-Letter Word* (1965).

3 From pupil in *Blackboard Jungle,* Sidney Poitier became teacher in *To Sir With Love* (1967), where he faced mini-skirted and unruly pupils like Lulu and Judy Geeson, seen here getting a talking to from director James Clavell.

2

3

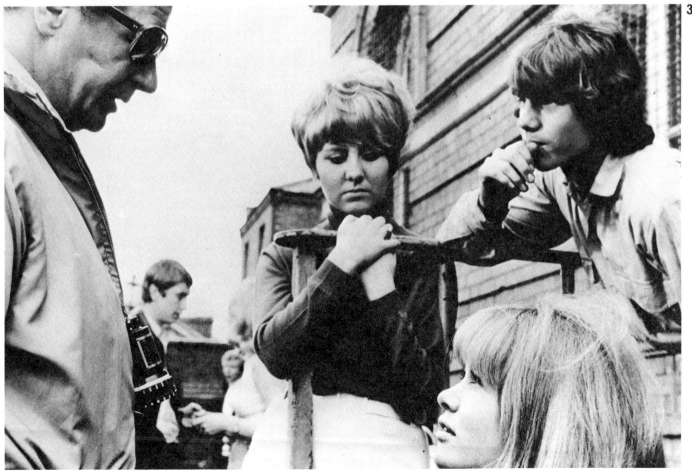

London had stopped swinging by 1966, but who would have known? The myth was alive and well and living in the movies.

1 Alfie (Michael Caine), the philandering East-End Lothario, possessed an insatiable appetite for the ladies. Here he rejects a main dish of Lancashire Hot-Pot, in the form of the sweet and tidy Annie (Jane Asher), in favour of hot potato Ruby (Shelley Winters). Directed by Lewis Gilbert, *Alfie* (1966) also included a flock of sixties birds from Millicent Martin through Shirley Anne Field, to Eleanor Bron and Julia Foster.

2 Dynamic duo Rita Tushingham and Lynn Redgrave hit town for a *Smashing Time* (1967) and soon found it all too much. They weren't alone.

3 Dennis Waterman and Suzy
(Sloane Ranger) Kendall propose a
toast to Adrienne Posta.
4 Not just a pretty face, Lynn
Redgrave in the title role of *Georgy
Girl* (1966) endured manic
reassurance from Alan Bates.

1 David Hemmings got the right exposure in Michelangelo Antonioni's *Blow Up* (1967).
2 *Girl on a Motorcycle* found Marianne Faithfull riding Naked Under Leather.

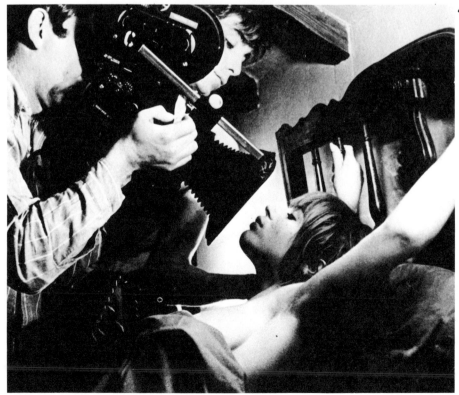

3 Between takes: the ex-convent schoolgirl is seen on the right track inhaling the mountain air.
4 Back on the job, Jack Cardiff's fully extended bellows catches Marianne mid-way through an asthma attack.

Performance was directed by
Nicholas Roeg and Donald Cammell
in 1968, but because Warner Bros
failed to understand its avant-garde
flavour, it gathered dust on the shelf
for a further two years before its
general release.
1 East End villain Chas Devlin (James
Fox) surveys the view in the mews
before submerging in the gloomy
decadence of Turner's (Mick
Jagger's) bolt-hole.
2 Mick, all lips and leather, paves
the way for John Travolta.

1

2

3 Bathtime for Turner, a ménage à trois that was one of the hot scenes that gave Warner Bros cold feet.
4 Baby it's cold outside. Turner helps Devlin out of the closet. The soundtrack featured Randy Newman, Ry Cooder, Buffy Sainte-Marie, The Last Poets and Mick singing "Memo from Turner".

CATCH A WAVE: Celluloid surfin'

Ho-dads, hot doggers, kooks, wipe-outs, glassy sets, woodies, custom machines and beach bunnies — this was pre-hippie teenage America as Hollywood saw it. The beach movie became for many a celluloid hallucination of teenage Utopia, an endless summer where even the bad guys were good and there were two girls to every boy.

Surfing had been a growing recreation along the West Coast since George Freeth, the Celtic-Hawaiian surfing pioneer, first introduced the sport to California in 1907. The sport's popularity was helped enormously in the early fifties by the introduction of Bob Simmons' lightweight or Malibu board. This easy-to-handle board helped so much that by the end of the decade surfing had become a way of life for many of Southern California's teenagers.

About this time, Californian film maker and surfing enthusiast Bruce Brown (who rode his first wave at the age of twelve) released his first full-length surf movie, *Slippery When Wet* (1959). The movie attracted great interest among California's surfing population. His following increased with his second release *Barefoot Adventure* (1961), but it was his third movie that finally won him international acclaim and prompted *Time* magazine to describe Brown as "a Bergman of the boards". *The Endless Summer* (1966) featured two surfers, Mike Hynson and Robert August, in a mythological search for the perfect wave.

Producers over at Universal were quick to see the commercial possibilities of this fast growing cult and soon signed teen star Sandra Dee for the title role in the forerunner of all the beach movies *Gidget* (1959). Directed by Paul Wendkos, *Gidget* also starred Cliff Robertson and teen idol James Darren. Robertson's interest in surfing went beyond his movie role, as he once explained: "One day, production on the picture got held up while we waited for a shipment of boards to come in from Honolulu and I got thinking why couldn't the West Coast support a surfboard industry. Certainly the sport had progressed beyond the fad phase. So with a partner, I set up a small operation in Venice, California." The Robertson Surf Board Company was soon producing a hundred boards a week and were not only wholesaling along the West Coast but as far afield as Florida, Peru and back to Hawaii.

Another young actor in the movie, Doug McClure, also took an interest in the sport and became a keen surfer, while James Darren signed for the sequel *Gidget Goes Hawaiian* (1961), this time featuring Deborah Walley in the title role. By 1961 surfing had become a complete teen sub-culture incorporating not only movies but its own style of dress, language, publications and music.

Surf guitarist Dick Dale and his group the Deltones gained a huge local following playing weekend dances at the Rendezvous Ballroom, Balboa, Southern California. A 4000-strong crowd would attend the venue each night, while his 1961 Los Angeles Sports Arena Concert found 21,000 fans in search of 15,000 seats. Although Dale only managed to score a couple of minor national hits, this ardent local following became a mini legend, as influential writer Tom Wolfe once observed, "Dick Dale is pretty popular among the kids out here because he sings a lot of 'surfing' songs." Without splitting hairs, the best of Dick Dale's surf music was anything but sung; in his own words "Real surfing music is instrumental . . . characterized by heavy staccato picking on a Fender Stratocaster guitar, and it has to be a Stratocaster." This unique style not only earned Dale the tag "King of the Surf Guitar", but also a major role in AIP's long-running beach party series, until ill-health and contributing problems forced him into an early retirement.

In the year that *Gidget* turned her back on the beach society in *Gidget Goes to Rome* (1963), American International Pictures waxed their clapper boards, jumped in their woodies and headed on out to Malibu to catch a wave that would last a hundred reels.

From its conception in 1954 AIP's movie policy, under founders James Nicholson and Sam Arkoff, was aimed directly at the teenage market. Their first massive hit, *I Was A Teenage Werewolf* (1957), grossed an estimated $2,000,000 in the US alone. They also encouraged the talented Roger Corman who produced around fifty of AIP's movies in ten years, including the highly respected Edgar Allan Poe series. The beach movie became yet another lucrative extension of their existing movie philosophy.

Under the skilful direction of William Asher the series hit the screen with *Beach Party* (1963) and incorporated a basic concept, cast and crew that hardly changed from one movie to the next. Frankie Avalon, who portrayed the series' romantic lead, once remarked: "I've made *Beach Party* and *Muscle Beach Party*, and the next one is *Bikini Beach Party*. After that I guess it'll be *Son of Beach Party*." It wasn't; the producers eventually agreed on *How to Stuff a Wild Bikini* (1965), a choice that ruffled a few feathers down at the British Board of Censors who quickly changed "Stuff" to "Fill" but that's about all.

Annette Funicello, who portrayed Frankie's long suffering beach-blanket bunny Dee Dee throughout the series, had been a famous child star. Discovered by Walt Disney at a children's ballet recital, she became chief Mouseketeer in the long running *Mickey Mouse Club* TV show (1955/59). She continued her career at Disney's via a number of feature films and a string of hit records that included "Tall Paul" and "Pineapple Princess". It was this latter success that won her a spot on the 1958 coast-to-coast Dick Clark Caravan of Stars Show. However, it wasn't until her agent Jack Gilardi negotiated her *Beach Party* role that she finally shook off the mouse ears forever. Wholesome Annette went into marriage and semi-retirement in the late sixties and has told reporters since: "I get scripts that would have me on dope, raped or getting an abortion. I'm just not interested."

AIP had one final dip in the ocean with *Beach Blanket Bingo* (1965), then tried a new location in *Ski Party* (1965), substituting snow for surf and Asher for Alan Raftkin. AIP didn't always have the beach to themselves, for by the mid-sixties others were exploring and exploiting the surf 'n' pop genre, which partly explains their switch from surfboards to snow skis.

Of the others *Surf Party* (1964) from Fox came close to the AIP formula. It too employed a cast of exiles from the hit parade — on this occasion Bobby Vinton (who claimed only to have received $750 for his appearance) and Jackie De Shannon headed the gang. The only other obvious ingredient that differed was its use of black and white stock and the less slick direction of Maury Dexter, who followed with *Wild On The Beach* (1965), featuring Russ Bender.

The Girls On the Beach (1965) stood out from the crowd only because it was the Beach Boys' one and only beach movie appearance. The Beach Boys were beyond doubt the biggest name to survive the surf era. The group were all teenagers living in Hawthorne, a Los Angeles suburb, when they released their first disc "Surfin'" in December '61. The disc hit the national charts hot on the heels of two other surf records, Dick Dale's biggest chart success "Let's Go Trippin'" and The Marketts' "Surfers' Stomp". The reason why the Beach Boys broke away, leaving many, including Dick Dale, in their wake, was the enormous talent of chief Beach Boy Brian Wilson for songwriting, arranging and producing. Wilson not only wrote two of the best songs in the movie, including the title song and "Little Honda", but also contributed songs for other beach epics, including *Muscle Beach Party* (1964) and the title song for Don Taylor's *Ride the Wild Surf* (1964).

Surf music's dynamic duo Jan and Dean took "Ride the Wild Surf" high up the charts and were originally due to co-star with Fabian in the movie. However, after a notorious bit of mischief they were dropped in favour of Tab Hunter and Anthony Hayes. Jan and Dean did get one consolation — the movie's leading teen starlet Shelley Fabares wrote a humorous sleeve note for their "Ride the Wild Surf" album.

Shelley was a Santa Monica schoolgirl, Michele Fabares, when she got her first showbiz break as a dancer on a Frank Sinatra TV show. She soon graduated to TV acting and not long after made her movie debut in *Never Say Goodbye* (1956), quickly followed by *Rock, Pretty Baby* (1956) and its sequel *Summer Love* (1958). Between movies she portrayed Donna Reed's TV daughter in *The Donna Reed Show*. Then, in 1962, she gained a million selling disc success with "Johnny Angel". More hit records, more movies, including a couple of Elvis vehicles, and more TV roles followed, and took her beyond the teen star label.

Jan and Dean did make a movie appearance hosting the pop

concert pic *The Tami Show* (1964) which also featured the Beach Boys. The Beach Boys appeared on screen again in Disney's *The Monkey's Uncle*, aiding AIP's queen of the beach bunnies, Annette Funicello, with the title song.

Directed by Robert Stevenson, *The Monkey's Uncle* also starred another Disney favourite, Tommy Kirk. Kirk, a late arrival on the surf 'n' sand scene, joined Annette over at AIP for *Pajama Party* (1965). He later rode the genre out with two highly forgettable splashers — *Catalina Caper* (1967), originally entitled *Never Steal Anything Wet* — a piece of advice he must have ignored when signing for the later *It's A Bikini World* (1967). For to all concerned, the movie turned out to be a complete disaster and even prompted its director Stephanie Rothman to confess, "I became very depressed after making *It's A Bikini World."* However, Tommy wasn't the only established teen star to dip his career in the ocean.

To the unsurfy sounds of The Supremes singing the title song and "Surfer Boy", TV's Ed "Kookie" Byrnes bounced through Lennie Weinrib's *Beach Ball* (1965), helped along by "A beachload of talent!" including Chris Noel and The Hondells.

Another member of a surf music duo (Bruce and Terry), Terry Melcher (who also happened to be Doris Day's son and heir) teamed up with Bobby Darin to write the score for Jack Arnold's *The Lively Set* (1964) which featured a song performed by the Surfaris of "Wipe Out" fame. The movie starred James Darren and Pamela Tiffin who were also seen in *For Those Who Think Young* (1964) the same year.

Back on the ski slopes (which had become almost as crowded with film crews as the beach) we were offered *Winter A Go-Go* (1965) with the Hondells, among others, *Wild, Wild Winter* (1966) and to round off the decade the stranger-than-fiction *Last of the Ski Bums* (1969). Strange, for it was promoted as being made by the same team that produced *The Endless Summer*, although it was directed by Dick Barrymore and featured Ron Funk, Mike Zuet and Ed Ricks.

The wave of beach party pics wasn't all sunshine and ho-dads, in fact they found their biggest critics within the surfing community. They blamed surfing's pop-culture for destroying their precious lifestyle by over-popularizing their sport and beaches, as illustrated in *Pacific Vibrations* (1970). Directed by *Surfer Magazine's* publisher, John Severson, it examined the problems caused by overcrowding on some of surfing's favourite spots. For the record, during the surf boom Severson had made an album on Capitol Records, home of Dick Dale and the Beach Boys, that in its way had contributed to the problem.

Leaving the exploitation and controversy aside, perhaps *Life* magazine summed up the beach set and genre best when it included within the December '69 special these profound words: "The rewards of exuberant health and youth, timeless realities of any age, still lie in the curl of a wave".

1 The Four Preps throw caution to the wind in this wild and uninhibited scene from *Gidget* (1959).
2 From *The Guns of Navarone* to the big gun boards of *Gidget Goes Hawaiian* (1961), James Darren puts a brave face on it. Co-starring in the title role is Deborah Walley.

3

4

5

3 *Gidget Goes Hawaiian* also found
Michael Callan peddling paddles on
beach at Waikiki. Former dancer
Callan (Martin Caliniff) once revealed
how he came to take his first steps
into showbiz: "When I about twelve or
thirteen I was at a party with a little
girl named Maxine. She was doing the
Charleston and I didn't know how, so
she gave me a lesson right there.
About five years later I got my first
job in a Broadway show – because I
could Charleston." He was later to trip
the light fantastic as a teen heartthrob
through a string of movies including
Because They're Young (1960), *Bon
Voyage* (1962), *The Interns* (1963) and
the TV series *Occasional Wife*.
4 Annette grits her teeth in anticipa-
tion of the gratuitous pie-fight finale in
William Asher's *Beach Party* (1963).
The plot to this forerunner of the
successful AIP beach series was
something out of pure pop art
Americana. Frankie (Frankie Avalon)
plans a moonlight serenade with Dee
Dee (Annette Funicello), but his
scheme is all but wiped out when she
arrives with the rest of the gang
including Deadhead (Jody McCrae)
and Johnny (John Ashley). Frankie
retaliates by faking a romance with
local beach vamp (Eva Six) and then
the trouble really gets underway.
Others on the sidelines of their sandy
haven include a sympathetic anthro-
pologist nicknamed Pig Bristles (Bob
Cummings) who observes their antics
as part of his research into teen tribal
customs, bad beach bully and ho-dad
Erick Von Zipper (Harvey Lembeck)
and surf music band Dick Dale and
the Deltones.
5 Just when we thought it was safe to
go back into the water . . . Life begins
at forty fathoms and ends in the hotel
pool in this scene from Del Tenny's
The Horror of Party Beach (1963). The
reviewers called it "horrible" and
"half witted", the producers simply
billed it as "the first movie monster
musical".

1

2

3

4

"Biceps, Bikinis, Surf and Sun, Music, Lovin' and Beach Time Fun" proclaimed the posters for *Muscle Beach Party* (1964), the second of William Asher's seashore scene-setters.

1 Dick Dale, "King of the Surf Guitar", drives a wedge between Frankie Avalon and Annette Funicello.
2 Down at Cappy's Surf Club, Dick Dale, "The Pied Piper of Balboa", plays second fiddle to Little Stevie Wonder.
3 Surf City grinds to a halt as Candy Johnson, a tastefully turned out temptress, trips a tasselled tango. This step was officially titled the Ebb 'n' Flow.
4 In a break from shooting, a damp Dick "Surfers' Choice" Dale relaxes with a couple of kittens.

1 Harvey Lembeck played Erick Von Zipper the perennial bad beach bully, throughout the series. In *Bikini Beach* (1964) Erick psychs out Frankie, Dee-Dee and the gang.
2 America's bald and messy answer to Britain's long-haired but clean-cut Beatles, the Pyramids made their film debut and departure in *Bikini Beach*.

3

3 The tide was on the way out for yet another Bill Asher surf splasher with *Beach Blanket Bingo* (1965).
4 In *How to Stuff a Wild Bikini* (1965), two members of the cast succumb to the soporific effects of a bottle of Coppertan suntan lotion.
This was, perhaps not surprisingly, the last of William Asher's sunny, sandy, soppy shindigs.

4

5

6

1 As the sun set on the beach movie formula, the cast took to the slopes for its successor. In *Ski Party* (1965) the Hondells fight a rearguard action before they too swopped surf for snow.
2 Though heavily disguised as a Christmas cracker, James Brown still cut an incongruous figure on the *Ski Party* slopes.
3 Deborah Walley and 4 Lesley Gore perform under the supervision of *Ski Party* song instructor Gary Usher.
5 "No it's *my* stick," protests James Stacey in off-camera antics during the making of Richard Benedict's *Winter A Go-Go* (1965).
6 The Astronauts land another cameo in Lenny Weinrib's sensationally tedious *Wild, Wild Winter* (1966).

1 "But you promised me a go!" A Bobby Vinton and Kenny Miller confrontation in Maury Dexter's full bed and board *Surf Party* (1964).
2 The Routers let go with "Crack Up" in their *Surf Party* cameo.

3

3 Blanket frenzy in William N. Whitney's *The Girls on the Beach* (1965) and a plot that went from here to eternity.
4 The Beach Boys made their one and only safari into celluloid surf with *The Girls on the Beach,* providing the title track and some curiously self-effacing acting.

4

1

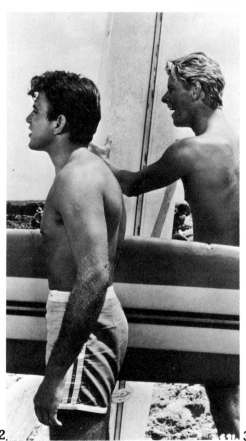

2.   3

1 "Anybody know how to work these things?" asks Tab Hunter in Don Taylor's *Ride the Wild Surf* (1964).

2 In the same movie, Big Jim Mitchum describes how he came to make a vertical landing.

3 In search of the perfect wave, baggy-clad Fabian and Peter Brown eye up a glassy set in *Ride the Wild Surf.*

4 "The nicest surprise to happen in the low budget movie business in a long-time" – *Life Magazine.* "Breathtaking! sweeping and exciting" and "One of the year's ten best films" – *Newsweek.* "An uncritical ode to sun, sand, skin and surf. Audiences everywhere, surfbored by the dry run of Hollywood beach party musicals, may relish the joys of summer!" – *Time.* This is how the big three summed up the dazzling surf spectacular *The Endless Summer* (1966). Written, photographed, produced, directed, edited and narrated by Bruce Brown, the movie used up some 50,000 feet of colour film, enough to run continuously for twenty-four hours. It was finally edited down to 91 mins 22 seconds of stoked surfing action.

5 Brown shot from a surfer's eye view to capture Californian hotdoggers Mike Hynson and Robert August in their 35,000 mile surfin' safari around the world.

6 Bruce arrives in Hawaii to be garlanded by none other than the legendary champion surfer Duke Kahanamoka.

1 The crash of the waves and the roar of the surf are a long way from the Hollywood back lot and studio tank. Scenes from the making of Leslie Martinson's *For Those Who Think Young* (1964): Scene 1, Take 1 – who waxed James Darren's board? Take 2 – A helping hand. Take 3 – I think I'm going to be sick. Scene 2, Take 1 – One of the cast makes a break from the sandy frantic antics. **2** All summer long Bobbi Shaw has fun, fun, fun in Don Weis' *Pajama Party* (1964).

3 Doug McClure and Pamela Tiffin take hot-rodding literally in *The Lively Set* (1964), directed by Jack Arnold.

4 Down at the Disney sock-hop rehearsals are under way for the opening scene of *The Monkey's Uncle* (1965), directed by Robert Stevenson and co-produced by Ron Miller.

5 "I'd suggest a 54C cup", says Sharon Tate in *Don't Make Waves* (1967). Based on Ira Wallach's book *Muscle Beach*, the film was directed by Alexander Mackendrick and also starred Tony Curtis and a soundtrack featuring The Byrds.

Filmed at the Tami Awards Show at Santa Monica Civic Auditorium on the 29th October 1964, this movie has been exhibited under various titles such as *The Tami Show, Teenage Command Performance* and *Gather No Moss.* Directed by Steve Binder and filmed in Electronovision, it was a pot-pourri of musical styles.

1 Jan and Dean, the surf duo, MC'd proceedings with much gusto and skateboard athletics.

2 The Beach Boys sang "Surfin' USA", "I get Around" and "Dance, Dance, Dance". A rare treat to see Brian Wilson perform with the boys.

1

2

3

3 Introduced in the title song as "coming from Liverpool", London's Rolling Stones, together with Gerry and the Pacemakers and Billy J. Kramer and the Dakotas, were representatives of the growing British invasion.
4 James "King of them all, y'all" Brown leads the Famous Flames through a set including "A Prisoner of Love", "Please, Please, Please" and "Night Train".
5 Detroit's soul sophisticats, the original Supremes, purred through "Baby Love" and "Where Did Our Love Go" with their inimitable sensuality.

4

5

THE FABS ON FILM:
Scream & scream again

The Beatles were to the sixties what Elvis had been to the fifties. Their music crossed all frontiers and the personal style and tastes of John, Paul, George and Ringo were closely followed and copied by their fans. If the Fabs grew moustaches, then moustaches were in; if they were hooked on the mystic, then mysticism was the thing.

They possessed a musical genius for keeping pace and usually one step ahead of the field. When the Beach Boys released their big production number "Pet Sounds", many thought that the Californians had finally out-gunned the Liverpudlians, but the Beatles just turned-on and put out "Sergeant Pepper", taking an unsuspecting rock world by storm. They also managed to top the whole San Francisco hippie scene by releasing undoubtedly the best flower power anthem of the era, "All You Need Is Love", with a B-side including such lyrics as "How does it feel to be one of the beautiful people".

The Beatles were for the better part of the sixties *the* beautiful people, and to remind us all of just how splendid it all was we thankfully have them on film. . .

The first British group to break American rock dominance, the Beatles were to the '60s what Elvis had been to the '50s.

Their movie debut, *A Hard Day's Night* (1964), was an enormous commercial success. Crammed with cinematic gags, it influenced a stream of British films, whose feverish whimsy far outreached their modest daring. But in 1964 it was a breath of fresh air – Swingin' London had arrived!

3

Screenwriter Alun Owen studied their speech and behaviour and created a script around 36 hours of their lives. John's performance as the happy anarchist and Ringo's melancholy loner stand out, along with the magnificent seven songs on the soundtrack.

1 and **2** If I Fell; John and George in yet another Beatle leap session.
3 Similar stills were used as part of the film's TV studio set design.
4 On the set, the Beatles pose with director Richard Lester. Lester, director of such earlier pop and comedy movies as *The Running, Jumping and Standing Still Film* (1959) and *It's Trad, Dad!* (1961) contributed greatly to *A Hard Day's Night's* energy, inventiveness and fast-paced humour.
5 Running, jumping and standing still, the Beatles epitomized in *A Hard Day's Night* the zany optimism of their time.

5

1 Out on a windy Wiltshire plain
Paul, the left-handed gun,impresses
George and Ringo with his prowess.
John's sights are set on Ascot.
Originally entitled *Eight Arms to
Hold You,* the movie finally surfaced
as Dick Lester's *Help!* (1965).
2 The sound of some 50,000
Beatlemaniacs challenges that of the
four Mop-Tops . . . The Beatles lost,
as was documented in the concert
movie *The Beatles at Shea Stadium*
(1966). Filmed in August 1965 at New
York's famed open-air sports venue.
3 Transcendental T-shirt, instant
meditation, "John you been a
naughty boy. George – you let your
trips go mod" – Dr Timothy Leary. Just
four spaced-out ex-military band
members taking a coach ride to a
Boxing Day TV movie that was almost
their Waterloo. Directed by the
Beatles, *Magical Mystery Tour* (1967)
when first screen was universally

1

2

3 slammed by the critics. New York's *Village Voice* called it a "home movie" that "came over as a calculated affront to professionalism", yet today it stands as an almost charming psychedelic curio.

4 Jeremy shows the Fab Four the way to Pepperland via the *Yellow Submarine* (1968). Based on John and Paul's song of the same name, the movie featured some fine animation by Heinz Edelmann, slick direction by George Dunning and witty screenplay by Lee Minoff, Al Brodax, Jack Mendelsohn and Erich *(Love Story)* Segal . . . plus, in a brief finale, the Beatles.

4

No longer the Fabs, the Beatles showed all the signs that within the confines of their collective structure lay four highly individual talents Michael Lindsay-Hogg and his cameras recorded the metamorphosis in *Let It Be* (1970).
1 "When I find myself in times of trouble . . ." coos Paul.

2 The movie gave George a wide choice of leads.
3 John gazes across the universe in a brief break from the orbiting oriental.
4 "You and I have memories" . . . but is that enough to keep the other three awake?

2

3

4

LET IT ROCK: Here's the scene we all joined in

The mid-sixties was a teenage watershed — a period of change and adjustment, an era when the now generation convinced themselves that they were on the road to a new explanation, through a growing indulgence in drugs, free love, happenings and civil rights and anti-war demonstrations. In the midst of this great re-evaluation of old modes and tastes, the well groomed teen idol got the rocket, to be replaced by not so well groomed rock heroes ...

If one event clearly marked the high point of the sixties rock revolution, then that honour must fall to the 1967 Monterey International Pop Festival in those crazy, heady days of summer, beautiful people, love-ins, flower power, psychedelia and "Sergeant Pepper's Lonely Hearts Club Band".

Fortunately for posterity D.A. Pennebaker was around with hand-held cameras to capture the festival as a movie feature that later emerged under the title *Monterey Pop* (1969).

The festival film, as the event itself, was a fine pot-pourri of mid-sixties rock and pop styles and stars. It was even rumoured on the day that the Beatles had arrived. "They are here, but they are disguised as hippies," announced ex-Beatle press officer and festival organizer Derek Taylor with a fine example of his tongue in cheek word play. Taylor's witticisms had taken him from the *Hoylake and West Kirby Advertiser* to the West Coast of America as press agent to the stars and on to become a main communicator at Apple Corps, a record producer and a legendary record company executive in only one thin autobiographical novel entitled *As Time Goes By*.

Discounting Rolling Stone Brian Jones, who is observed on film pretending to be just one of the crowd, The Who finally turned out to be the only completely UK act to make an appearance. However, they made up for it with an abrasive performance attacking stage and equipment in true frenzied form that climaxed in customary Who devastation.

The soul representative, Otis Redding, certainly had the audience on his side, winning the hearts and ears of the hippie audience with his "love crowd" patter and magnetic personality — a great performance by a great showman that sadly turned out to be one of his last, for he was to die tragically a year later in an air disaster.

Other beautiful people who brought their special magic to the moment and movie included Jimi Hendrix (making his US debut), Simon and Garfunkel, Janis Joplin, Country Joe and the Fish, Jefferson Airplane and the Mamas and the Papas.

The mid-sixties witnessed another unique rock music experiment in the Monkees' TV series. The group was pieced together, Magnificent Seven fashion, from an ad placed by TV producers Robert Rafelson and Bert Schneider. These young, good-looking, zany and individually talented Beatle clones included ex-TV *Circus Boy* child star Mickey Dolenz, long tall Texan Mike Nesmith, folkie Pete Tork and former British juvenile TV actor David Jones. This new form of rock packaging produced not only the highly successful TV series but a string of chart hit singles and albums plus an overlooked (at least by many moviegoers) feature-movie, *Head* (1968).

Other pop stars of the day who appeared in less than successful movie ventures included Harry Nilsson as a prison guard in Otto Preminger's *Skidoo* (1968) and Paul Jones in Eric Sykes' *The Committee* (1968).

Nilsson had a much better time with his next couple of movie outings. The first was his version of Fred Neil's song "Everybody's Talkin'" which was chosen for the *Midnight Cowboy* (1969) soundtrack. The choice was made by director John Schlesinger thanks to Derek Taylor who had played him Nilsson's Aerial Ballet album at a party. The second, *The Point* (1971), was an even greater undertaking, for Harry not only conceived the original idea, wrote the story and composed all the songs, but he even developed a highly original sales technique — he followed an American TV executive aboard a plane and sold him the movie in mid-flight. The film turned out to be a highly original children's animated fantasy directed with great style by Fred Wolf and narrated by Dustin Hoffman.

Hoffman had only acquired movie stardom a few years earlier portraying Benjamin, a guy who was a little worried about his future and a certain Mrs Robinson in Mike Nichols' *The Graduate* (1967). He later confirmed his growing superstar status in the role of Ratzo the street-wise hustler in *Midnight Cowboy*.

Nilsson's own acting career took a downward slide when he played the title role in the rock-horror movie *The Son of Dracula* (1974) but his record sales took an upward turn, scoring with a handful of singles and the series of highly acclaimed Nilsson Schmilsson albums, the last of which was produced by one Derek Taylor, plus the soundtrack to Robert Altman's *Popeye* (1980).

Paul Jones fared little better in his movie career, achieving his greatest movie moment opposite Jean Shrimpton in *Privilege* (1967), the first in a short line of semi-political pop features.

Not only were rock stars adding pulling power to the movies, but rock music was also playing an increasingly important part in their content. Groups like the Zombies, Lovin' Spoonful, Simon and Garfunkel, Harper's Bizarre, and The Association were adding credit songs, party music and general background sounds to the screen action of the films such as *Bunny Lake Is Missing* (1965), *What's Up Tiger Lily* (1966), *The Graduate* (1967), *I Love You Alice B. Toklas* (1968) and *Goodbye Columbus* (1969). Perhaps the best use of contemporary rock music in a movie was the selection compiled for *Easy Rider* (1969). It included some of the best in rock of the day by Hendrix, Dylan, the Byrds, The Band and others.

Easy Rider also put Jack Nicholson's career into top gear. He had been around the movie industry for some years, mainly as an actor in Roger Corman's teen-horror pics, but also contributing to film scripts including *The Trip* (1967), the vehicle that originally featured *Easy Rider*'s Peter Fonda and Dennis Hopper together, and the Monkee movie *Head* (1968). *Head* marked his first collaboration with Monkee inventor Robert Rafelson who went on to direct Jack's *Five Easy Pieces* (1970). Nicholson's drop-out, cop-out, opt-out characters have continued to rear their familiar heads throughout his career, his most famous and successful being Murphy in *One Flew Over the Cuckoo's Nest* (1975), which was based on a book by beat novelist Ken Kesey.

Italian director Michelangelo Antonioni covered some of the same ground as *Easy Rider* in his first American production *Zabriskie Point* (1970), famous for the intro-outro screen careers of leading stars Mark Frechette and Daria Halprin. Frechette portrayed a Los Angeles student on the run after a campus riot ends in the death of a policeman. This everyday funky revolutionary student steals a plane and heads out across the desert only to meet sympathetic hippie secretary (Halprin). Halprin, on her way to join capitalist boss at a business meeting, indulges in some choice "let's change the system" dialogue, a bout of uncomfortable love making (ever crunched sand in your sandwiches?) and a spot of airplane painting. After so much fun, Mark flies the expropriated craft back to the city only to be shot by the Los Angeles Police Department. Daria on the other hand carries on to her conference that ends in a mighty pop-art explosion.

A much bigger pop explosion was filmed the same year in upper New York State on Maxie Yasgur's 600-acre farm near the usually tranquil village of Bethal. Hordes of spaced out rock followers followed one another up the freeway to the venue for that celebration of love and peace that became known as *Woodstock* (1970). The spirit founded at Monterey reached a climax and was abandoned at Woodstock in an extravaganza billed as three days of Peace and Music; fortunately the movie only lasted 184 minutes. It did go some way in furthering the reputations of Monty exiles Hendrix, The Who and Country Joe, while also featuring Santana, Joan Baez, Joe Cocker, Crosby, Stills and Nash, John Sebastian and Arlo Guthrie among others.

Guthrie had achieved a unique movie success the previous year appearing as himself in Arthur Penn's *Alice's Restaurant* (1969). The film was based on the extracts from Arlo's own life and experiences that had first surfaced in the song of the same name, a movie venture marking the first ever film to take its plot from a rock song.

Back at Woodstock where an estimated 300,000 turned up, tuned in and turned on, Janis Joplin was heard to burp "even Billy Graham doesn't draw that many people".

A harassed Woodstock organizer had pleaded "If we're going to make it, you had better remember that the guy next to you is your brother!" This hip sentiment was forgotten by the Hell's Angels policing the Rolling Stones free concert at North California's Altamount Speedway as they bludgeoned a young black to death, an act that was graphically captured in *Gimme Shelter* (1970). This incident, coinciding with the abandonment of the hopeful sixties, finally undermined the hippie-flowerpower philosophy, rendering it a spent force as the major youth movement. A counter culture had always co-existed with the peace and love movement, producing a stream of exploitive, violent box office crowd-pullers that included *A Fistful of Dollars* (1964), *Bonnie and Clyde* (1967), *Easy Rider* (1969) and *A Clockwork Orange* (1971). It was reported that the Rolling Stones had taken an option on the film rights of Anthony Burgess' nightmarish *Clockwork Orange* novel but they let it slip, and it was left to Stanley Kubrick to bring the futuristic rape and murder drama to the screen.

On the straight rock movie front, the behind the scenes concert tour packages gained an enthusiastic audience, the most popular of the genre following the cinema verité style of D.A. Pennebaker and his mini-masterpiece *Don't Look Back* (1965). This highly respected piece of celluloid captured Bob Dylan in mood and performance during his 1965 UK tour, but the warts-and-all treatment proved too much for the folk hero who never permitted the ensuing movie, *Something Is Happening*, to be generally released. Dylan was later seen in *The Concert for Bangladesh* (1972) helping Beatle buddy George Harrison raise cash aid for the newly formed state and its refugees at a star-studded benefit held at Madison Square Garden.

New York was also the backdrop to a very different kind of movie, *Shaft* (1971), the first and probably the best in a genre of semi-exploitive vehicles introducing new black actors to the screen. Richard Roundtree portrayed private investigator John Shaft doin' his thing while struttin' his stuff to the Oscar-winning score supplied by Isaac Hayes. Hayes also played the title role in the highly exploitive *Truck Turner* (1974) and around the same time guested in a couple of episodes of *The Rockford Files* TV series. Roundtree as Shaft also found a second home on the small screen, but not before two further big screen outings in *Shaft's Big Score* (1972) and *Shaft In Africa* (1973).

Movies and heroes aimed at the teenage market were gradually being integrated into the general cinema scene, titles such as *Shaft* (1971) and Dylan's *Pat Garrett and Billy the Kid* (1973) although containing a strong rock culture element were nevertheless appealing to a much wider audience and age group. It took a young, highly-gifted school of filmmakers to turn the clocks back some twenty years to revive rock in the aisles and teen idols on the screens.

Produced by Lou Adler and Papa
John Phillips and directed by D. A.
Pennebaker, *Monterey Pop* (1969)
distilled the essence of the
psychedelic phenomenon. Forty-five
hours of 16mm footage was edited
down to a powerful and compact 79
minutes of rock history.

1 An overwhelming rendition of "Ball
and Chain" was delivered by the
hard driving, hard living and
irreplaceable Janis Joplin.

2 Eric, the white man's Burden, leads
the Animals through "Paint It Black".

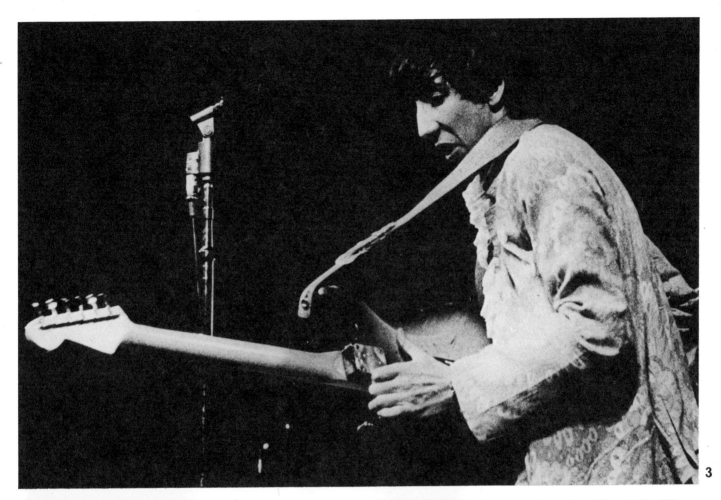

3

4

3 Pete Townshend leads The Who through "My Generation" to its customary but none the less devastating climax.
4 Country Joe, the hippy's hippy in full flower.

1 Paul Jones as the evangelical Government-puppet-pop-idol in Peter Watkins' meandering *Privilege* (1967). The movie also starred the Vogue-style beauty Jean Shrimpton.
2 Mind the cameraman! – the Monkees in *Head* (1968). Directed by Bob Rafelson, the movie owed a lot to Jack Nicholson's cinematic genius and Dick Lester's Beatle movies.

3

3 Dennis Hopper, star and director of *Easy Rider* (1969), once confided "I've got to act in my movies because I love acting, because I'm really good at it and I never really had a chance to show it. I've always had to take shit and make gold out of it. And now I've got gold and they're trying to make shit of it." Helping Denny to make gold or . . . Jack Nicholson and Peter Fonda.
4 In *Alice's Restaurant* (1969), Arthur Penn took Arlo Guthrie and his talking folk blues song of the same name as main ingredients for his personal view of '60s hippie spirit and ideology.

4

1 He'll always remember graduation day . . . Mrs Robinson (Anne Bancroft) seduces young Benjamin (Dustin Hoffman), who with good reason looks a little worried about his future in Mike Nichols' tasteful *The Graduate* (1967). The movie also featured Katherine Ross as Elaine Robinson and a well received soundtrack from Simon and Garfunkel and Dave Grusin.

2 Super-stud Joe Buck (Jon Voight) had a soft spot for Brenda Vaccaro in *Midnight Cowboy* (1968). Directed by John Schlesinger the film gave Dustin Hoffman the opportunity, as Ratso Rizzo, to establish himself as one of the decade's leading actors.

3 Francis Ford Coppola's *You're A Big Boy Now* (1967). Nineteen-year-old knock-kneed New York Library employee (Peter Kastner) attempts to break away from his over-protective parents and becomes infatuated by a callous young actress (Elizabeth Hartman). John Sebastian and the Lovin' Spoonful supplied the sound-track.

4 An armada of real ducks circle around Richard Benjamin and Ali MacGraw during their picnic in *Goodbye Columbus* (1969). Directed by Larry Peerce the movie marked the screen debut of the very dependable Benjamin.

Director Ken Russell left the classical composers to rest in peace while he turned his elaborate attention to Pete Townshend and The Who's rock-opera *Tommy* (1975), for which he also contributed the screenplay.

1 All decked out in fifties fashions Nora (Ann-Margret), deaf, dumb and blind Tommy (Barry Winch), and Frank (Oliver Reed) depart for Bernie's Holiday Camp.

2 Tommy (Roger Daltrey) is given Nora's helping hand to touch the statue of Marilyn in the shrine dedicated to her deification and her power to heal the afflicted.

3

3 Poised to receive the multi-shot in the arm, Tommy stands inside the Acid Queen's (Tina Turner) baco-foil Iron Maiden.
4 Pete leads Keith and John through the classic "Pinball Wizard" sequence.

4

1

1 *Woodstock* (1970) – "Three days of
peace and music. Hundreds of acres
to roam on. Walk around for three
days without seeing a skyscraper or
a traffic light. Fly a kite, sun yourself.
Cook your own food and breathe
unspoiled air." The best of
Woodstock was captured on film by
director Michael Wadleigh and
edited down by Martin Scorsese to a
long 184 minutes.
2 Decked-out in whirling spaghetti
Roger Daltrey led The Who through
an abrasive set at the gargantuan
youth outing that *Time* magazine
called "history's biggest happening!"

2

3

3 The unmistakable invisible guitar playing of Joe Cocker, who shone brightly at the "Aquarian exposition".
4 Honkin' down the highway – the *New York Times* wasn't so enthused by the great tribal gathering and labelled it "an outrageous episode" and went on "what kind of culture is it can produce so colossal a mess?"

4

1 "The music that thrilled the world . . . and the killing that stunned it!" *Gimme Shelter* (1970) – the Rolling Stones documentary directed by David and Albert Maysles and Charlotte Zwerin – included the notorious Altamont murder of Meredith Hunter by a pack of Hell's Angels policing the Speedway concert.

2 Described as "a film made purely as a piece of rock and roll entertainment", *Born To Boogie* (1972) focused on the glittering king of teeny bop, Marc Bolan, and his Wembley Concert. Directed by Ringo Starr the movie also featured an appearance by Big-Daddy, Elton John.

3 Joe Boyd, John Head and Gary Weis directed *Jimi Hendrix* (1973), in a compilation of some of Jimi's concert footage and TV appearances, with interviews that collectively stand as a fine epitaph to one of rock's highly respected innovators.

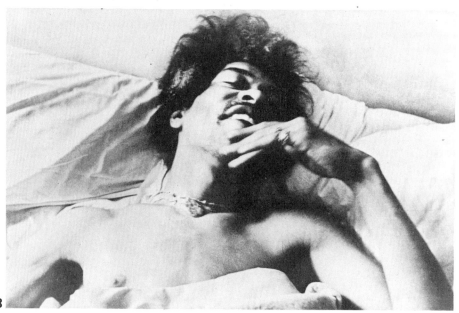

ACT NATURALLY: The media monsters

In recent years the title superstar has been bestowed on many in such a throwaway fashion as to render it almost meaningless. There are, however, a special few who deserve this accolade — Presley and the Beatles certainly, and also the individuals profiled here. They are the great crossovers, the ones who have achieved artistic and commercial success on both disc and in the movies . . . the real Superstars.

Mahogany's ebony queen Diana Ross.

Ringo Starr (Richard Starkey)

After his successful wistful wanderings in the Beatles' first celluloid outing *A Hard Day's Night* (1964), most critics felt it was only a matter of time before Ringo would launch himself into a major solo movie career. Unfortunately his screen roles to date have lacked the early promise of that unforgettable cinematic moment.

1 Ringo as the Mexican gardener takes the iron maiden (Ewa Aulin) from behind in Terry Southern's zany sex satire *Candy* (1968), directed with much confusion by Christian Marquand.

2 Directed by Joseph McGrath, *The Magic Christian* also included young Dickie Attenborough, Peter Sellers in the role of the world's wealthiest man, and a soundtrack by Badfinger and Thunderclap Newman.

3 Once aboard the lugger, Raquel Welch takes Ringo's arm while inspecting the topless small bit players (seated), in Terry Southern's insane satire *The Magic Christian* (1970).

4 Dressed firmly in a polo-ribbed sweater our ex-Beatle portrayed Frank Zappa, leader of the intellectual outfit the Mothers of Invention, in a directionless and pointless waste of video-tape transferred to celluloid titled *200 Motels* (1971).

1

2

3

4

Bobby Darin (Walden Robert Cassotto) (1936-73)

Dick Clark once said of Darin, "I used to laugh when people told me how Bobby was an arrogant little son of a bitch. But if you knew him, he was the kindest, gentlest person. He had a great native intellect, and if he was only healthy physically, he probably could have gone on to be a legend." Bobby Darin was undoubtedly a true showbiz enigma – from his early rock 'n' roll hits including "Splish Splash", "Queen of the Hop" and the Louis Armstrong inspired "Mack the Knife", through his own successful songwriting to his superb screen acting. Bobby's ambition was to be a legend by the time he was twenty-five, a dream that somehow was never quite realized.

During his heyday, Darin could always be relied on for some great copy. When asked "Do you want to be as big as Sinatra?" he replied "No, I want to be the biggest Bobby Darin I can be, the best Bobby Darin in the world", and he didn't stop there, he went on "I hope to be the biggest in the world, be bigger than Sinatra."

In 1960 he married every freshman's fantasy, Sandra Dee, with whom he had a son, Dodd. Six years later their marriage ended in divorce. His second marriage, to Andrea Yeager, only lasted six months and they divorced just a month before Bobby's untimely death from heart failure, following some eight hours of open heart surgery at LA's Cedars of Lebanon Hospital.

1 "Bottoms-up," says Rock Hudson in a scene from Bobby's debut movie, Robert Mulligan's *Come September* (1960) – the first of three movies in which he co-starred with Alexandra Zuck, better known to many as Sandra Dee.

2 Bobby and leading lady Stella Stevens seem unimpressed by director John Cassavetes' display of fisticuffs during the shooting of *Too Late Blues* (1961).

3 American Nazi psychopath (Darin) and ace baddie Richard Bakalyan discover a new format in the shape of Mary Mundy, for a quick game of tic-tac-toe in *Pressure Point* (1962).

4

5

4 Action-packed director Don Siegel describes how to hitch a ride between scenes of the rugged war drama *Hell is for Heroes* (1962). Darin fared extremely well in the company of co-stars Steve McQueen and James Coburn.

5 In William Hale's *Gunfight in Abilene* (1967), Bobby portrays a gun-shy sheriff who is forced into taking up arms against a gang of Hollywood outlaws. This sagebrush opus also included Bobby singing his own composition over the credits.

6 Unsuccessful gigolo ((Darin) shares one for the road with the mature Jean Simmons in Richard Brooks' bitter sweet *The Happy Ending* (1969). Sadly, the film marked Bobby Darin's final exit, a great loss made even more poignant by Michel Legrand's title theme "What Are You Doing the Rest of Your Life?"

6

Art Garfunkel

After the successful teaming of Simon and Garfunkel's music and Mike Nichols' visuals in *The Graduate,* it wasn't very long before Art Garfunkel was working with the talented director again, but this time in front of the cameras.

1 He made his dramatic debut in Mike Nichols' screen version of Joseph Heller's *Catch 22* (1970) or "No sane man would wish to fly, therefore anyone wishing to stop cannot be insane". Garfunkel as Lieutenant Nately shoulders Yossarian's (Alan Arkin) unsurmountable problem.

2 Art was teamed with Jack Nicholson in Mike Nichols' *Carnal Knowledge* (1971), where they portrayed two college friends whose enthusiastic and varied sex life develops into a discontented middle-aged obsession.

3 As an American psychoanalyst with a new style of bedside manner, he comforts emotionally-unstable Viennese housewife Theresa Russell in Nicolas Roeg's *Bad Timing* (1980).

1

2

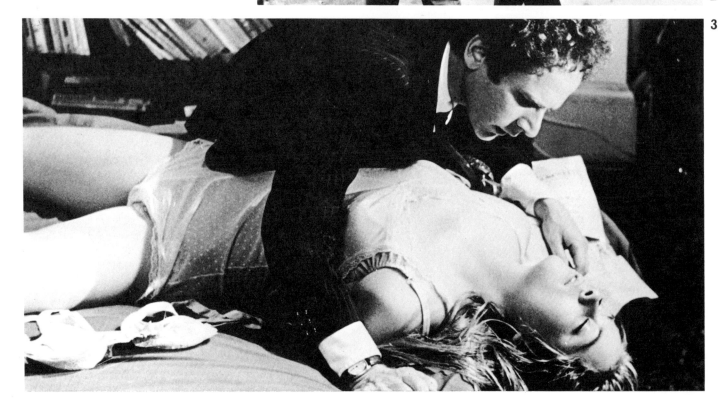

3

4

David Bowie

4 The flamboyant David Bowie (formerly David Jones) added a further dimension to rock music by injecting some high theatre into his stage act with a galactic array of mime and make-up. This special image added credence to his first major movie role as Thomas Jarome Newton, the fallen angel in Nicolas Roeg's dazzling yet pretentious sci-fi excursion *The Man Who Fell to Earth* (1976).

5 David Hemmings' *Just A Gigolo* (1978), a story of everyday Prussian folk in Christopher Isherwood's Berlin, found Bowie in the company of Sydne Rome (slouched left) and Maria Schell making the connections. His scene with Marlene Dietrich was not shot independently and later edited together. Following his big screen success Bowie once again took to the boards, this time taking Broadway by storm in the title role of the 1980 stage production *The Elephant Man.*

5

David Essex

After years in the wilderness performing with unheard of groups and playing small parts in unmentionable movies, David Essex finally made it, and how . . . On stage he became a hit in *Godspell* and the sensation of *Evita,* on record he produced a string of hit singles, on television he starred in his own short but effective series and in the cinema he was one of the leading teen dreams of the seventies. This latter success was due mainly to his role as Jim MacLaine in two vehicles that protrayed in some way the story of rock.

1 David as a lounge lizard helps Ringo prop up the bar in *That'll Be The Day* (1973).
2 Dave watches intensely as Adam Faith de-fleas the bedroom rug in *Stardust* (1974).

1

2

3

Kris Kristofferson

Burly Texan Kris Kristofferson had some lean years before Roger Miller recorded his "Me and Bobby McGee" – then all sorts of hell let loose. More major recording stars covered his material, including Johnny Cash and Janis Joplin, and he acquired his own gold disc with "Silver Tongued Devil" and "I", plus a movie cameo role in Dennis Hopper's less than successful *The Last Movie* (1971). Within a few years Kris had not only become a million selling singer and songwriter but a massive box office attraction to boot!

1 About to put his cards on the table a chubby cheeked and clean shaven Kris as William Bonney faces Pat Garrett (James Coburn) in Sam Peckinpah's deadly dull *Pat Garrett and Billy the Kid* (1973). The movie led at least one critic to write "Boredom reigns supreme in retelling the Western saga of Sheriff Garrett going after ex-crony Billy the Kid". The project wasn't helped by co-star Bob Dylan whose original music score made as much impact on the film as Custer at the Little Big Horn.

2 Kris played piggy-in-the-middle between George Segal and Susan Anspach in Paul Mazursky's "funny-sad love story" *Blume in Love* (1973).

3 All touch and no feel seems to sum-up the third remake of William Wellman's inspired *A Star is Born* (1937). In this 1976 version, set against the world of rock music, Kris and Barbra Streisand were third best in the roles previously portrayed by Frederic March and Janet Gaynor, and James Mason and Judy Garland.

Diana Ross

Diana Ross, the supreme Supreme, won an Academy Award nomination for her debut movie Sidney J. Furie's *Lady Sings the Blues (1972).* Sadly her subsequent film engagements have failed to attract as much attention.

1 A couple of trendy indoor gamers join the theatre audiences in catching 109 winks as Diana and Tony Perkins go through the paces and transparencies in Berry Gordy's *Mahogany* (1975), a film noted for the departure of director Tony Richardson mid-way through shooting.

2 Diana gritted her teeth and looked jolly uncomfortable riding high and wild as Dorothy in *The Wiz* (1978). Directed by Sidney Lumet the movie was a black musical version of the 1939 classic *The Wizard of Oz* featuring Judy Garland.

3

Twiggy (Lesley Hornby)

3 After years of being the world's number one clothes peg, Twiggy hit the screen in Sandy Wilson's charming twenties pastiche *The Boy Friend* (1971), directed by Ken Russell with his customary light touch.

4

Bette Midler

4 The divine Miss Midler burst upon the movie scene in *The Rose* (1979). Directed by Mark Rydell it won her an Academy Award nomination for the role of a Janis Joplin-style drugs and booze lady of the blues.

John Travolta once summed up his career by saying, "I just hope I'm never restricted . . .!" Featuring in a string of rapid-fire rock inspired movies, Travolta won the hearts of young girls almost everywhere. Born on 18th February 1954 in New Jersey, Travolta's road to stardom took him from stage musicals such as *Bye Bye Birdie, The Boy Friend* and *Grease,* through minor movie and TV roles, most notable being Brian De Palma's *Carrie* (1976) to the role of Vinnie Barbarino in the TV series *Welcome Back Kotter.* It was this latter role that caught the attention of producer Robert Stigwood who was looking for a leading man to portray the macho bum-wiggler in *Saturday Night Fever* (1977). The role established John as a star and he soon capitalised on this enormous success with an even bigger one, the film version of *Grease* (1978). It was *Grease* that launched his chartbusting career with such hits as "You're The One That I Want" and "Summer Nights" being culled from the soundtrack.

1 Electric blue eyes and dimpled chin, hallmarks of John Travolta's huge screen appeal.
2 It was back to school for the Hollywood classroom soapa *Welcome Back Kotter.*
3 Macho 'n' movin' with Karen Lynn Gorney in John Bradham's gutsy *Saturday Night Fever* (1977). The movie helped resurrect the Bee Gees' career in giving them the vehicle to showcase their distinctive disco sound.
4 Riding high on the *Grease* (1978) wave, he was bound to fall – it came, and how, in *Moment by Moment* (1979). Although he soon climbed back in the saddle for James Bridge's mechanical *Urban Cowboy* (1980).

1

AISLE JIVIN' REVIVIN': This is where we came in

It had been almost twenty years since Bill Haley's teenage anthem, Rock Around the Clock opened *Blackboard Jungle*. From the rhythm of its backbeat a movement was born, a generation tuning in and turning on to the grand illusion of a rock 'n' roll world.

Without it we might never have witnessed Presley, *The Girl Can't Help It*, Mamie Van Doren, Fabian, *Because They're Young*, Tuesday Weld, Cliff, *G.I. Blues*, the Twist, Kookie, Shelley Fabares, beach movies, Beatlemania, Dylan, the Rolling Stones, Soul, Otis, *A Hard Day's Night*, the Monkees, Twiggy, Hendrix, hippies, *Monterey Pop*, Tiny Tim, *Easy Rider, Woodstock*, Bowie and John and Yoko. Then, when such good times seemed all over, and oldies thought it safe to go back into the cinema, it all came flooding back. Pounding over the credits came that same infectious beat, and once again the aisles were in the jivin' business — but this time the piper took the form of possibly the greatest teen movie to date, *American Graffiti* (1973).

Directed by George Lucas, *American Graffiti* was more than enthusiastically received by critics and rock fans alike — " . . . a boisterous bumper-to-bumper ballet . . . Lucas has captured a moment recognizable to every generation" (Paul D. Zimmerman, *Newsweek*). "Superfine" (Jay Cocks, *Time* magazine), and " . . . magnificently acted, edited, directed, photographed and scored" (Rex Reed, *New York Sunday News*). Even I, when reviewing the movie for *The Story of Pop*, called it "a boss nostalgic movie" (boss was later changed to great, at the editor's insistence). These are just some of the plaudits granted to Lucas and his fine young cast — a cast that was headed by a relative newcomer to movies, Richard Dreyfuss, who played Curt.

Brooklyn-born Dreyfuss moved with his parents to California in 1956 where he attended Beverly Hills High School. At the tender age of fifteen he acquired an agent and was soon appearing in many popular TV series including *The Big Valley* and *Mod Squad*. Movie roles soon followed, including a two-line part in *The Graduate* (1967), a cocky car thief in the restless teen opus *The Young Runaways* (1968) directed by Arthur Dreifuss, and a kid in the soggy underwater comedy *Hello Down There* (1968), directed by Jack Arnold.

But it was *American Graffiti* that really put his career on the map, and when his next movie, Ted Kotcheff's *Apprenticeship of Duddy Kravitz* (1974), hit the screen most critics were praising Richard Dreyfuss as "the finest American film actor since Brando". This was worthy acclaim for the actor who went on to star in *Jaws* (1975), *Close Encounters of the Third Kind* (1977), *Whose Life is it Anyway* (1982), not forgetting his Oscar-winning performance in Neil Simon's *The Goodbye Girl* (1977).

American Graffiti was also instrumental in the careers of its other talented young actors. Paul Le Mat, who played John Milner, a heavy-lipped hot-rodder in the James Dean/Fabian mould, went on to star in *Aloha, Bobby and Rose* (1975) and *Harold and Frank* (1980), among others. Candy Clark, whose character Debbie owed a lot to the Sandra Dee/Connie Stevens school of frock 'n' roll, later played a very different role opposite David Bowie in *The Man who Fell to Earth* (1976). More surprising was Harrison Ford's later success in *American Graffiti*. Ford had the minor roll of Bob Falfa, pretender to Milner's auto crown, but he went on to become a leading light in the Lucas stable, heading *Star Wars* (1977) and *The Empire Strikes Back* (1981), and Steven Spielberg's *Raiders of the Lost Ark* (1981). Ronny Howard (Steve) and Cindy Williams (Laurie) became biggies on the small screen, Cindy starring in *Laverne and Shirley*, a spin-off of Ronny Howard's highly popular *Happy Days* series, itself a direct descendent of the great *Graffiti*. Most of the cast reassembled for the less-popular sequel *More American Graffiti* (1979) proving that the original had offered a touch more than mere nostalgia.

The nostalgic TV series *Happy Days* introduced the world to a new teenage cult hero, the Fonz, a character taking some of its inspiration from *Sunset Strip's* Kookie. Fonzie was portrayed by the likeable Henry Winkler, who had already cut his teeth in the rock revival arena, portraying a member of a 1957 New York street gang in Stephen F. Verona's *The Lords of Flatbush* (1974), a movie that also featured the acting and screenwriting talents of Sylvester (Rocky) Stallone.

John Travolta, a then up-and-coming teen screen idol, was also considered for the highly prized Fonzie role — a difficult choice for the show's producers who must have been ultimately swayed by Winkler's interpretation of H-e-y. However, Travolta soon earned his chance to display the Brylcreem bounce in Randal Keiser's movie *Grease* (1978).

Grease had started out as a 1972 Broadway stage musical. Douglas Watt writing about the Eden Theater production said: "The charm of *Grease* is its ability to capture the innocence and joy of a new pop-culture manifestation", and went on to say that it was very modest in its aims and very sure about them. It succeeded because of the simplicity of its theme and because of the calculated skill with which it was presented. The original musical score was written by Jim Jacobs and Warren Casey. The show's touring cast included the young John Travolta, who six years later found himself portraying the lead in the movie version opposite the lovely Olivia Newton-John. The film also featured a couple of Hollywood's oldest teenagers, Frankie Avalon and Ed Byrnes.

Grease was another fine example of a growing trend in rock 'n' roll nostalgia movies, a genre that also helped make David Essex a star. Essex, the lead of the London stage production *Godspell*, quickly became an overnight blue-eyed sensation, partly through his series of hit discs, but mainly via his characterization of Jim MacLaine, the rock 'n' roll runaway in Claude Whatham's *That'll Be The Day* (1973). In this film, which was set in late-fifties England, David inserted just a hint of Dean's cool and McCartney's melancholy that complemented perfectly the film's other leading character Mike, portrayed by Ringo Starr.

The movie also featured a couple of marvellous cameos by the late Billy Fury as the holiday camp rock singer, Stormy Tempest, and Keith Moon as his drummer. Moon supplied one of the best tongue-in-cheek lines of the movie — when asked by MacLaine why they didn't write their own songs, he replied "Only Americans can write songs".

Keith Moon once again joined David Essex for the sequel *Stardust* (1974), but this time Ringo Starr was conspicuous by his absence, leaving many believing that perhaps the film was a bit too close to the truth for comfort, as the storyline dealt with Jim MacLaine's eventual rise to fame with a Beatle-inspired sixties rock group. Ringo's role was taken over by scene stealer Adam Faith, who was joined by contemporaries Marty Wilde and Ed Byrnes.

The Beatles themselves became victims of the nostalgia boom and were aped and impersonated with varying degrees of authenticity, from Michael Shultz's vaudeville fantasy *Sgt. Pepper's Lonely Hearts Club Band* (1978) and Richard Marquand's early years biopic *Birth of The Beatles* (1979) to Joseph Manduke's filmed stage show *Beatlemania* (1981).

Other interesting rock 'n' roll revival movies that beg to be mentioned include *Let The Good Times Roll* (1973), a well edited blend of vintage movie clips and newsreel footage, set against a couple of Richard Nader's popular rock revival concerts featuring such survivors as Bill Haley, Fats Domino, Little Richard and Chuck Berry. Berry again appeared as his own rockin' self in the biopic of Alan Freed, *American Hot Wax* (1977).

Interest in the early rock music legends continued with a host of film biographies including *The Buddy Holly Story* (1979) and *Elvis — The Movie* (1979). Meanwhile TV movies offered the Jan and Dean story via *Deadman's Curve* (1978) starring Richard Hatch, Bruce Davison and Beach Boys Mike Love and Bruce Johnstone, and *James Dean* (1976), with a solid performance by Stephen McHattie as the ill-fated young star.

Since his tragic death, James Dean had also been the subject of a couple of documentary movies including *The James Dean Story* (1957), which was partly directed by Robert Altman, and *James Dean — The First American Teenager* (1975), narrated by Stacy Keach with contributions by Dennis Hopper and Dean's one-time co-star, the soon-to-be-murdered Sal Mineo. There has also been a series of morbid pop songs dedicated to his memory with titles such as "The Ballad of James Dean" and "His Name was Dean" and a few reasonable tributes such as the Beach Boys' "A Young Man's Gone" and The Eagles' simply-titled "James Dean".

Nostalgia continued to flourish through the late seventies, moving on from rock 'n' roll's golden era of the fifties to the beat of the sixties. Among the many, we were offered *The Wanderers* (1979), directed by Martin Ransohoff and starring Ken Wahl and Karen Allen, which was yet another everyday story of a New York street gang.

Sixties England was revisited via Franc Roddam's *Quadrophenia* (1979). Based on The Who's concert album of the same name, it starred contemporary rock stars Phil Daniels, Sting and Toyah Wilcox in an authentic reconstruction of the world of Mods and Rockers. Sting (Gordon Sumner) the Ace Face in the movie and The Police, had previously appeared in a few television commercials before landing the part. Following the success of his debut movie he caught the acting bug and soon turned up in the role of an auto-mechanic with an Eddie Cochran fixation in Christopher Petit's *Radio On* (1979). Apart from continuing his musical career he is now firmly established as a screen actor, appearing in the BBC TV production *Artemis 81* and the movie *Brimstone and Treacle* (1982). Other new idols had appeared from the world of television and included David Cassidy of *The Partridge Family* series, who didn't quite come to terms with his sudden and enormous success, and David Soul of *Starsky and Hutch* fame, who did.

David Soul (or Solberg) was straight out of the established tradition of young actors using their massive small screen popularity to launch themselves into a subsidiary pop music career. However, David proved he wasn't just another flavour of the month as he moved from movie roles, such as his portrayal of John Davis, the killer rookie in Clint Eastwood's *Magnum Force* (1973), through his TV success, to the pop singles and album charts with equal drive, talent and commitment.

The punk scene spawned a new breed of teen idol. Although many offered little more than their youth, they caught the imagination of countless restless teenagers, who were very much in need of their own image and hard-up heroes. One of the bigger new wave bands, Blondie, quickly gained a much wider acceptance, thanks mainly to the pouting good looks of their lead singer, Debbie Harry. Debbie, who was raised in New Jersey, was once asked how the band came by their name — "Blondie was a street name I got from truck drivers," she explained, "they always yell 'hey Blondie, hey Blondie'." With the looks of a teenage queen in the Monroe/Bardot mould, it wasn't very long before she was seen in the movies. Her first role was that of a frustrated wife in Mark Reichert's offbeat crime drama *Union City* (1980).

With the eighties rock stars such as Debbie Harry and Sting making sorties into celluloid, Rockerama should live for at least another twenty-five reels and maybe another twenty-five years.

George Lucas' *American Graffiti* (1973) opened at Mel's Drive-In, Burger City, the local hangout for the town's teenagers somewhere in California's sun-drenched Central Valley. The background of the movie is reminiscent of the first great teen movie *Rebel Without a Cause.* It tells the story of the last night of the summer vacation, when the four main characters – Curt Henderson, Steve Bolander, John Milner and Terry "Toad" Fields – will be together for the last time, before Steve and Curt fly east to college the following morning.

The film follows the boys and their girlfriends from dusk to dawn in a teen ritual that includes cruisin' the streets to the sounds of Wolfman Jack's XERB radio show, jivin' at the high school sock-hop, makin' out on the river bank while under the influence of Old Harper, drag racing on deserted dawn-lit country roads, until the finale at the airport the following morning.

Rex Reed summed up the film best when he wrote "This is the best movie about kids in small-town America since *Red Sky at Morning* and an absolute must for anyone who has as much nostalgia about growing up in the late 1950s and early 1960s as I do!"

1 Curt (Richard Dreyfuss) is press-ganged by the Pharoahs, Joe (Bo Hopkins) and Carlos (Manuel Padilla Jr), who seem to be having trouble deciding who's gonna have the longest ciggie.
2 To the strains of the Big Bopper's "Chantilly Lace", Badass (Johnny Weissmuller Jr) attempts to rearrange Terry the Toad's (Charlie Martin Smith) good looks.

3 Following an auto accident during an illegal street drag-race Bob Falfa (Harrison Ford) is about to see stars as Laurie Henderson (Cindy Williams) strikes back.

4 Between hot platters and melting popsicles Wolfman Jack was heard to howl "Awwrigght, baay-haay-baay! I got a oldie for ya-gonna knock ya right on the folow-baay-haay-hee-baay!" among other platitudes.

5 Steve (Ronny Howard), Laurie (Cindy Williams), Debbie (Candy Clark) and Terry (Charlie Martin Smith) reunite for B.W.L. Norton's less successful sequel *More American Graffiti* (1979).

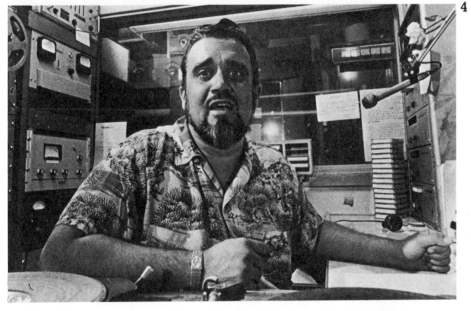

1 Paul Mace, Sylvester Stallone, Henry Winkler and Perry King as the '50s Brooklyn high school gang *The Lords of Flatbush* (1974). Directed by Stephen F. Varona and Martin Davidson, who also co-wrote the screenplay with Gayle Gleckler and the pre-"Rocky" Stallone. The movie included a soundtrack composed by Joe Brooks and featured a scene with the leather clad fraternity singing some fine do-wop street corner harmony.

2 Late for class nice Susan Blakely runs the gauntlet.

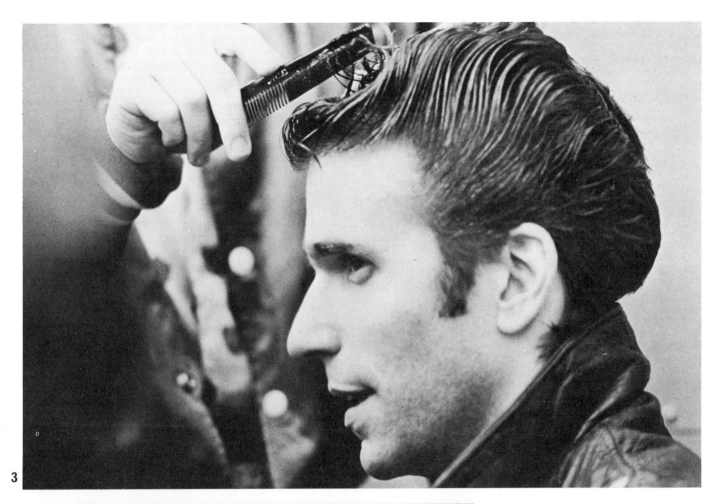

3 In *The Lords of Flatbush* Henry Winkler found an image he was to use again to become a household name . . . The Fonz.

4 The nurds of Milwaukee – TV's *Happy Days* was loosely based on *American Graffiti* and even starred one of its leads, Ron Howard, as Richie Cunningham (right), with Donny Most and Anson Williams flanking Fonzie.

1

Let the Good Times Roll (1973) was the last great rock 'n' roll revival package. Directed by Sid Levin and Bob Abel, the movie combined vintage '50s film clips with contemporary concert footage in an amazing jive down memory aisle.

1 Bill Haley tempted the Teds back into the aisles with "Rock Around the Clock" in this, his last major movie.

2 Rock of ages . . . Chuck Berry during his solid set that included "School Days", "Reelin' and Rockin' " and "Sweet Little Sixteen".

3 The provocative Little Richard injected high camp and acrobatics into his zestful performance.

4 Finding his thrill, the fabulous Fats Domino at the grand.

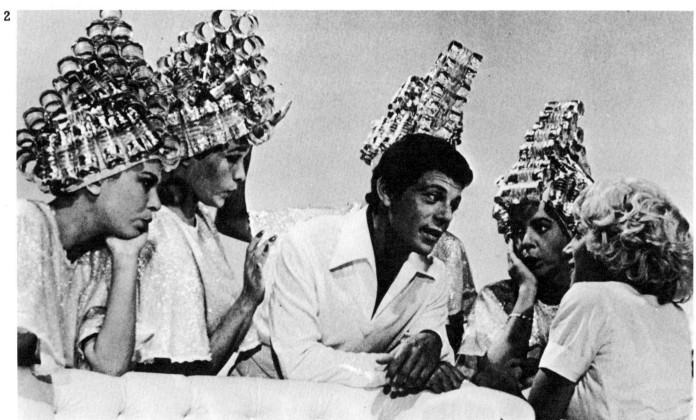

1 In a dazzling display of aerodynamics John Travolta leaves Olivia Newton John agasp as he wings his way across the floor in the most successful flight of nostalgia to date, Randal Kleiser's *Grease* (1978).
2 All curled up with a gang of matronly headbangers, Frankie Avalon crooned his way through "Beauty School Drop-Out" as if he'd never been gone.
3 Barely recognizable without his hot-rod and comb Ed "Kookie" Byrnes, who deserves a lot better, turned up for yet another cameo role.
4 John nibbles Olivia's lean and lovely lobes during the hit number "You're the One That I Want".

3

1 Steve Rath's biopic *The Buddy Holly Story* (1979) featured a highly believable performance by Gary Bushey in the title role and fine support by Charlie Martin Smith as the Crickets' stand-up bass player Joe Mauldin. Buddy Holly died tragically with the Big Bopper and Ritchie Valens when a plane carrying them crashed on 3rd February 1959. He remains one of rock 'n' roll's greatest legends.

2 Tim McIntire borrowed a jacket from Bill Haley to play Alan Freed in Floyd Mutrux's *American Hot Wax* (1977). Others taking part included (top) Jerry Lee Lewis and (left) Chuck Berry.

1

2

3

4

3 While Moon-the-Loon keeps the beat Billy Fury brings it all back home as Stormy Tempest, the holiday camp rock 'n' roll singer, in Claude Whatham's *That'll Be The Day* (1973).
4 David Essex shares a mike with Dave Edmunds who relived his Raider days at the Old Vic – Victorian Ballroom, Canton, Cardiff, that is – in Michael Apted's nostalgic *Stardust* (1974).

1

Man's love affair with the automobile
continued to fill the screen with more
custom-made car and rod movies.

1 *Two-Lane Blacktop* (1971),
directed by Monty Hellman, featured
a great performance from a '55 Chevy
and some pretty laid-back support
from Beach Boy Dennis Wilson with
Laurie Bird and James Taylor.

2 Jeff Bridges, one of the best of the
new screen actors, portrayed
stocker Junior Johnson in Lamont
Johnson's *The Last American Hero*
(1973). The movie was based on the
Esquire magazine story "The Last
American Hero is Junior Johnson
Yes!" by Tom Wolfe.
Son of Lloyd and brother of Beau, Jeff
Bridges has been hailed by some
critics as a new Wallace Beery. The
always dependable Bridges has
brought some choice characteriza-
tions to the screen via *The Last
Picture Show* (1972), *Thunderbolt and
Lightfoot* (1974), and *Tron* (1982)
among his many other movies
appearances. Jeff also became
involved in the rock documentary *The
Heroes of Rock and Roll* (1980),
hosting and narrating Malcolm Leo
and Andrew Solt's fine compilation
movie.

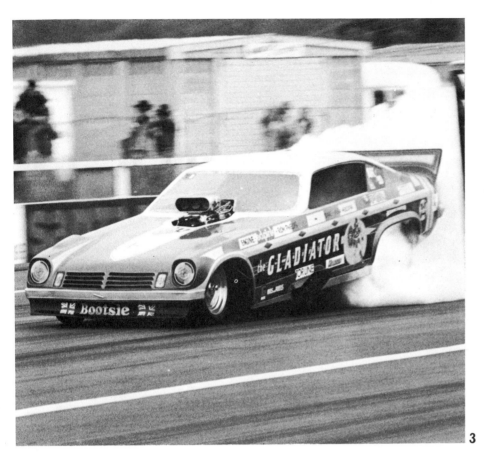

3 Making his second excursion into the UK hot-rod scene, American director Curtis Clark took his cameras and crew to Santa Pod Raceway for *Shut Down* (1978). At the drag strip he captured some spectacular race action and inter-cut this with some less successful fictional footage. The movie starred Brian Goodber, Lydia Lisle and Tim Cook but their performances were over-shadowed by a blown '57 Chevy and a primered Plymouth GTX, while over the screen action the sounds of the Beach Boys, Surfaris, Chantays, Super Stocks, Ronny and the Daytonas and others were heard, compiled by yours truly.

4 Another Californian teen sub-culture – surfin' – was revisited in John Milius' *Big Wednesday* (1978). The movie followed, in a moving and sometimes sensitive way, three surfer boys, Gary Busey, Jan Michael Vincent and William Katt, from 1962 to 1974.

1

Following the break up of the fab four, and amid speculation and rumour of Beatle reunions, a series of movies were produced celebrating the gear days of yesteryear.

1 The Rutles presented their own history of the Beatles in 90 minutes of paraodoxical nostalgia entitled *All You Need is Cash* (1978). Directed by Gary Weis and Eric Idle the film starred ex-Python Idle in the role of Dirk McQuickly, ex-Beach Boy Ricky Fataar as Stig O'Hara, ex-Bonzo Dog Neil Innes as Ron Nasty and John Halsey as drummer Barry Wom. The movie was helped enormously by Innes' original songs, capturing some of the spirit of the Beatles originals, and a fine script.

2 George Harrison heavily disguised as Derek Taylor interviews Rutle Corps press officer Eric Manchester (Michael Palin). Other celebrities

2

3 taking part include Mick Jagger, Paul Simon, Bianca Jagger, Penelope Tree and John Belushi.

3 Robert Zemeckis' *I Wanna Hold Your Hand* (1978) follows four New Jersey teenagers in their attempts to see the Beatles 1964 New York appearance on the Ed Sullivan show. Early Beatles songs heard on the soundtrack include "I Want to Hold Your Hand", "She Loves You" and "Please Please Me" among others.

4 The most disastrous Beatle-inspired flick to date was Michael Schultz's *Sgt. Pepper's Lonely Hearts Club Band* (1978). This star-studded waste of time included Peter Frampton as Billy Shears and the Bee Gees as the Band.

5 A group of semi-look-a-like actors were gathered together for Richard Marquand's pedestrian biopic *Birth of the Beatles* (1979). Produced by Dick Clark, the movie covered the Fabs' rise from Liverpool via Hamburg to their triumphant US television debut in '64.

1 The scooter boys head for the coast as The Who's generation take to the screen in Franc Roddam's homage to UK youth culture *Quadrophenia* (1979).
2 During a break between bank holiday battles Jimmy the Mod (Phil Daniels) demonstrates the latest discotheque step to a couple of laughing policemen.

3

3 Toyah Wilcox and Sting, lost in a sea of pork-pie hats, full-length leathers, surplus parkas and angry young faces, in the film that's been regarded by many as England's *Rebel Without a Cause*.

4 The Who's own history was documented in Jeff Stain's celluloid compilation *The Kids Are Alright* (1979). Contributors included Ringo Starr and Keith Richard.

4

Index

Bibliography

ATV Television Show Book. Purnell, 1962.

Belz, Carl, *The Story of Rock*. Oxford University Press, 1972.

Cummings, Tony, *The Sound of Philadelphia*. Methuen, 1975.

Halliwell, Leslie, *The Filmgoer's Companion*, 1976.

Life magazine, 1960-69.

Meeker, David, *Jazz in the Movies*. Talisman Books, 1977.

Murrell, Joseph, *The Book of Golden Discs*. Barrie & Jenkins, 1974.

Review Film Album. Spring Books, 1961.

The Rolling Stone Illustrated History of Rock. Random House, 1976.

Roxons, Lillian, *Rock Encyclopedia*. Grosset and Dunlap, 1969.

Speed, F. Maurice, *Film Review*. Macdonald, 1961.

Teen Screen magazine, 1959-61.

Wicking, Christopher and Vahimagi, Tishe, *The American Vein*. Talisman Books, 1979.

Wolfe, Tom, *The Kandy-Kolored Tangerine-Flake Streamline Baby*. Jonathan Cape, 1965.

Acknowledgements

The author gratefully acknowledges the kind help and assistance of Stewart Cowley, Charles Webster and EMI Records, Peter Campbell, Sarah Harman and United Artists, Debbie Bennett and Capitol Records, Peter R. Simpson, Moira Bellas and WEA Records, Charles and Bridgid, Maureen O'Grady and Decca Records, Lucy Williams and her cohorts deep down at the stills library – The British Film Institute, Cinema Internatonal Corporation, Columbia-EMI-Warner Films and the lovely Lizzie . . . Special thanks to Keith Bales and all at Walt Disney Productions, the Regent Cinema, Cardiff, Derek Taylor and Harry Nilsson.